IN HER OWN WORDS

Anne,
So glad to have you
in my life.
Love you
Ann

ALISON BRAITHWAITE

In Her Own Words

WOMEN'S WISDOM TO MOVE YOU FROM SURVIVING TO THRIVING

Lead by Nature
PRESS

Lead by Nature Press
www.AlisonBraithwaite.com
St. Catharines ON

ISBN 978-1-7750900-0-7 (paperback)
ISBN 978-1-7750900-1-4 (ebook)

Produced by Page Two
www.pagetwostrategies.com

Cover and interior design by Taysia Louie

Grateful acknowledgement is given to Judith Duerk for permission to reproduce an excerpt from *I Sit Listening to the Wind: Woman's Encounter Within Herself* by Judith Duerk (1993, 1999).

Printed and bound in Canada by Island Blue

18 19 20 21   5 4 3 2 1

*To the many women who have shared their stories, acted
as role models, and encouraged and inspired me in
my own becoming. May we continue to share our stories
and support one another's upward spiral of being and
becoming, of creating and re-creating ourselves.*

Contents

Foreword

BY LISA MCDONALD

I HAD THE HONOUR and privilege of being approached by Alison to write the foreword for her amazingly inspirational book. More importantly, I am both blessed and grateful to know this woman and call her friend, sister, and part of my tribe.

Alison definitely walks her talk, lives an impassioned life, and encourages others to do the same so as to maximize this gift we call life.

I have immense admiration and respect for Alison for the significant fact that she chooses to honour herself first and foremost. How she has learned to look after herself will become abundantly evident as you take the plunge with Alison on her raw, candid, and personal journey.

This is a must-read book! Thank you, Alison, for always extending your hand to others, me included, and for navigating us back to our individual sphere of core truth.

LISA MCDONALD
Internationally best-selling author, TV/radio show host, speaker, mentor, licensed and certified Passion Test facilitator, and life coach

1

IN MY
OWN WORDS

I IMPLODED. I BURNED out.

I craved supportive conversations that would move me forward, help me sort out what went wrong, and teach me the lessons I had missed along the way. Conversations that may have prevented this complete crumbling of who I was. The types of conversations I had previously experienced accidentally, I now wanted to intentionally create. I longed for meaningful conversations with women. I yearned to hear their stories and share the wisdom I received from them so that no one else had to experience the exhaustion and loss of self I was feeling.

I was the lone female executive for a highly successful company in Ontario, with operations across North America. I'd worked there for almost twenty years. Before that, I'd dreamed of working there. I had a clear, purpose-driven role: to look after the organization's environmental performance. The company operated within traditionally male-dominated industries: construction, waste management, chemical production, and quarrying.

I appeared to be the very definition of *success*. I had a good salary. I worked for a great company. As vice-president of environmental performance, I was making a difference. Yet I felt disconnected, defensive, and drained. I felt like I was working within a system that was not designed for me, with unwritten rules I did not understand. I was tired of trying to figure out those rules. I was tired of leaning into something that did not bring out the best in me. The passion for what I was doing had disappeared, and I was bored and restless. I looked around and saw a few amazing, articulate, intelligent young women starting to join the company. I loved mentoring them. They were passionate, alive, and energized. The exact opposite to how I felt. I felt misaligned, and I did not like how I was behaving as a result. I noticed how much these young women supported and appreciated one another. It was painful to acknowledge the contrast of our experiences. I longed for the support of compassionate colleagues and mentors, and I craved a reconnection to a sense of purpose. I cried my way to work most mornings, then put on a smile and soldiered on.

I started to reflect. What had gone wrong? What piece of wisdom had I missed that left me in a state of financially thriving but mentally and emotionally drowning? I was determined to find out.

What I discovered were the beliefs I had, some of which were limiting me:

1. **Everything is interconnected.** I was raised at the base of a mountain slope in North Vancouver with a stream running through, where nature was so integrated into life. At the age of six I had the opportunity to meet Chief Dan George and to hear him share Indigenous stories of interconnection, of honouring the earth, of respect. Respect for ourselves and where we come from, for the other beings that inhabit this earth, for those who came before us and those who are still to come. Chief Dan spoke of the tragic loss of what is being forgotten and the importance of planting seeds. He taught me to see the world as me and me as the world. He offered his stories to a room full of children: the sound of his voice beats on in my heart and his message lives on in my actions. That feeling of interconnection that was instilled in me was strengthened when I studied biology at university and formed the basis of the environmental performance program I created in the workplace.

2. **Sometimes I just have to trudge through things.** I was raised with this formula for happiness: get a university degree, find a husband while at university, get a good job, buy a house, and have children. By the end of high school, I was exhausted and bored with school and I knew I didn't want to go directly to university.

   My parents did not respond well to my desire to take a break from education. Going to university was an important step in their success formula. I love them both dearly and at seventeen was not able to express properly how I was feeling—totally burned out from school and in need of a rest. All I was able to do was resist. My resistance turned to acquiescence and I dragged myself to university to study biology. I chose biology as my major because it was my highest mark in my first year. I approached it half-heartedly looking for the path of least resistance, finding the easiest path, and expending as little effort as possible to complete the degree my parents so desperately wanted for me.

3. **I have to prove myself.** For my entire career as an environmental professional, I had been surrounded by men, by their impressions of other women, by their voices, and by their ways of doing things. Often I was the only woman in the room. It can be a lonely place, and I had changed myself in order to survive. When I was about twenty-three years old, I was a freshly hired environmental officer for Ontario's Ministry of the Environment. My responsibility at that time was hazardous waste. My partner in environmental crime-fighting was Dave. Our mission was to encourage businesses that generated hazardous waste to register their wastes with the government. The goal was to ensure that wastes were appropriately managed.

   We decided to provide weekly information sessions. Dave and I would help each other prepare the room and alternate who led the seminar. It was my turn to lead that week. Dave was setting up the projector and the screen. I was arranging the coffee. The participants were all middle-aged white men. When it was time to start, Dave walked out the door and I moved to the front. All eyes follow Dave as he left. There was panic in the men's faces as they watched Dave close the door behind him. Their body language changed as they realized I was leading the seminar. I could feel their bodies screaming, *What is this young chick going to teach me?* Dave was unquestionably accepted as having expertise. I had to earn that acceptance. I needed to prove I knew my stuff. I proved it in that room that day. By the end of the information session, I decided that I needed to work harder to have my abilities recognized.

4. **I have to shut down parts of myself to survive.** During a seminar, I was in a room full of seasoned environmental officers, all male. A woman stood at the front explaining the government's affirmative action program. When I think back, I realize how

difficult a role that must have been for her. At the time, I judged
her. My sense was that this woman in the pretty dress, with the
nicely manicured nails and bleached blond hair, with no technical background, was representing me as a woman and I could not
see me in her. The others in the room verbalized their judgments.
They were not happy with the possibility of women getting a
"free pass" into positions currently held by men. I was uncomfortable with the comments I was hearing, and although I could
not see myself in that woman, I could sense that the others in the
room did. I made a decision *not* to be her. To look too feminine
or to act too feminine would not serve me in my chosen career.
I shut down part of myself that day. I wonder how many other
decisions I have made in life that have shut down part of who I
am, that have separated me from a piece of who I am.

5. **Make friends with the hose.** When I started as an environmental
   coordinator in the private sector, I did what I knew. I taught environmental law, and when things went wrong I taught it again in
   more detail. I tried to understand a workplace that seemed to
   speak a different language than me. I felt like a foreigner in a
   strange land that was impossible to navigate. Within four years
   of joining the company, I was exhausted from trying. I questioned why I was there in the first place. I wanted to experience
   more of life. I wanted to learn Spanish and immerse myself
   in yoga. So I tried to quit my job by giving six months' notice.
   Instead, I was offered a leave of absence and accepted it with the
   intention of not returning. I headed to the cloud forest of Monteverde, Costa Rica, and then a yoga centre in Massachusetts.

   At the yoga centre, I learned an important life lesson, one
   that opened my mind and later transformed my approach at
   work. That change allowed me to create the cultural shift that
   inspired employees to "be" the environment at work and at
   home. I received room, board, and free yoga lessons in exchange
   for cleaning bathrooms and changing sheets. Being of service

in this way was surprisingly fulfilling. There was one bathroom I really did not like cleaning. It was in the basement and had floor-to-ceiling tiles. To clean those tiles, we needed to use a hose. I hated the hose. When I used that hose, I would end up with water and soap suds all over me. In that bathroom, I always volunteered to clean the toilets and the sinks so I wouldn't have to wrestle with the hose.

One fateful morning I was partnered with a guy (I think his name was Greg) who was a well driller. When I told him that I hated the hose and would prefer to clean the toilets, he was dumbfounded. He asked me why I didn't like the hose. I explained, "It's because I can't get the hose to do what I want it to do. I feel like I'm fighting with it all the time." Greg responded, "That's because you have to make friends with the hose. Nobody respects this hose. They just shove it back into the cupboard under the sink."

He walked over to the sink, opened the cupboard doors, and sure enough the hose was a tangled mess. He lovingly pulled it out from under the sink and gently allowed it to unwind itself in the way it needed to. Once the hose was stretched the full length of the room, he tenderly wound it in large loops. It was almost like the hose was guiding Greg on exactly how it wanted to be handled. The hose looked relaxed. Greg hung it on the half-wall by the sink. He used only a small section of it to rinse down the wall. It looked so easy. He asked me if I wanted to give it a try. I took the nozzle from Greg and was astonished by how easy it was to use. The hose was relaxed. I was relaxed. The bathroom walls and floors were cleaned effortlessly without the resistance of the hose and without me getting soaked. It was amazing.

I went back to work reluctantly after my eight-month leave of absence with no intention of staying. I planned to work for a few months to make a bit more money and then head to India to live in an ashram. That changed when I was given an opportunity to make friends with the metaphorical hose of my work. I was given twenty minutes to talk to a room of managers about how the environment was a pillar of the company. It was the perfect opportunity to change my approach to work.

That gift of twenty minutes to talk about the environment as a pillar of the company was the first time I brought my whole self to work. I felt vulnerable. I led the managers through a guided mediation. Connecting them to their breath. Inviting them to notice that as they breathed, they were borrowing from the environment and giving back. Inviting them to notice that in so many ways we are the environment and the environment is us. The culture shifted in that twenty minutes of me just being me and sparked a level of creativity that fed my soul for about seven years.

6. **I can do this on my own.** I lost the people who had helped to create the safe container for my creativity. I felt alone in a foreign land that was challenging to navigate, and my creative energy died. I found myself questioning if I was in the right place.

I wanted to feel alive, energized, and passionate again. I wanted to feel in "real life" what I felt when I was hiking the Himalayas or cycling in Patagonia. I wanted to routinely feel the sense of limitlessness and interconnectedness I had in nature. I wanted to thrive. I took a coaching course.

The coaching course was amazing. I was surrounded by people who wanted the best for one another, who believed in one another, and who deeply listened to one another. For the six months of the course, I was in heaven. I was working full-time, now as vice-president of environmental performance, and completing my coaching certificate. I felt so supported. Learning new things energizes me. Coaching shifted me into a sense of purposefulness for a while.

I wanted to explore something new. I wanted to find a way to create a workplace where everyone feels surrounded by people who want the best for them, believe in them, and really listen to them. I wanted to create a workplace that offered what I had found during my six months of studying coaching. And I wanted to do that with the guidance of women. I pursued my master's degree. It energized me to explore this concept.

After completing my master's, I found myself fighting with the metaphorical hose once again. It seemed to be a pattern for me and yet I was too misaligned with my work to reflect on that pattern.

7. **I can fix this, I just need to work harder.** I kept looking for a way to fix myself, to fix the work environment I found myself in, and nothing was working. I was moving further and further into a hole that I could not dig myself out of. It was time to try something different. I remember sitting in a circle with employees from the company and those from a company we had just acquired and being stunned at how passionately they spoke about our environmental performance program. In that circle, I understood the commitment to the environment that I had inspired and I was in awe of the effect I had had. Yet underneath that awe was extreme unhappiness. A few months later I quit my job, for good this time.

I wanted to find a way to create my world differently. I wanted to be part of making the world a kinder, gentler place where everyone felt recognized and celebrated for their uniqueness and where everyone felt a sense of belonging. Belonging was something I longed for and something I had strived to create my entire career. Yet I was not very aligned with kindness or gentleness. I was angry at myself and at others. What I longed for was to just be me, wholly and completely. It was time to look for answers beyond where I normally looked.

I remember hearing a story of shamans in Peru whose sole purpose (or perhaps *soul purpose* would be a better description) is to dream the world. It made me wonder who was dreaming our world? Who was dreaming the world I wanted to be a part of, and how did they go about dreaming it? When I reflected on who I wanted to talk with and what I wanted to learn, I thought back to that circle of women. I longed to hear women's stories.

I had spent almost twenty years with a company where I rarely felt wholly and completely me, and women's stories had been pretty much drowned out my entire career. I hadn't realized how much I needed to hear them until I read *I Sit Listening to the Wind: Woman's Encounter Within Herself* by Judith Duerk. The following passage revealed a deep sense of loss in me:

> How might your life have been different if, as a young woman struggling to find your voice . . . in despair that you might never be able to say what you knew inside . . . there had been a place for you to begin to speak as a woman?
>
> If you had been received into a circle of women, and during the silence, the women had let you speak . . . had let you speak over and over, as your words slowly came together. . . if they had listened deeply and attentively to your emerging voice?
>
> And, how might it have been different for you, if you had seen, that day, in the faces of the women sitting there in the circle . . . in the still older faces of the women standing slightly behind them in the shadows . . . the pride and respect they felt as they heard your young woman's voice?
>
> How might your life be different?

The tears rolled down my cheeks as I thought about how my life might have been different. I felt broken. I needed to find a way to shift from that deep sense of loss and grief to wholeness, and I understood that creating intentional conversations with women held the key.

I wanted to speak with women who were dreaming the world differently, women who were inventing and reinventing themselves.

I wanted to speak with women who believed in a different definition of success, one that wasn't just about financial striving but also about whole-self thriving, whole community thriving.

I wanted to hear stories that could prove it was indeed possible to shift into a thriving life. The thriving life I was looking for was the feeling I had when I stopped to do yoga alone in the Andes Mountains as I walked the Inca Trail. It is the feeling of limitlessness, connection, and a belief that everything is possible. Thriving to me is the sense of flow I felt when living in Monteverde, Costa Rica, where I was surrounded by nature, doing things that I loved with a community of incredible, supportive people. I lived completely in the moment, trusted I was looked after, and felt that life was effortless.

What I realize now is that thriving is about *being*. Our society seems to be about gathering information so we can get busy doing and then do more. But all that doing can get in the way of actually being. Being is where we connect with our unique gifts and blossom. Being is also a barometer—when you feel you can't be who you want to be where you are, it is time to reassess.

I wanted to understand whether I was the only one who had struggled when I was young. Was anyone else still trying to decide what to do for the rest of her life? Did those women who were creating their own way have really special parents or role models who recognized them and supported them from a young age? Did they have opportunities that I didn't? What might these women know that I did not know? How could their stories guide me and perhaps other women who were experiencing that same angst and uncertainty? I wanted to speak to role models who could provide a pathway into a fulfilling life, and I wanted to understand how other women have overcome inevitable obstacles.

I remember years ago sharing with a friend something I had dreamed of doing. She told me that I couldn't do it, which made me shrink inside. When I gave her a couple names of people who had already achieved this goal, she said, "Well, they are famous, of course they can do it." It made me realize that people see celebrities differently from how they see themselves, as if being famous granted them special abilities that the rest of us do not have. I wanted to interview relatable women, the women down the street who were making big differences in the world and yet were not celebrities, women who may not include fame in their definition of success.

My sense was that there is so much wisdom all around us that we just have to start asking questions about what we are truly curious about. Rather than talking about the weather, ask people about what really matters to them, find out what they are most proud of, or what they have learned from the mistakes they may have made along the way. Ask them about what may be keeping you stuck or about the direction you may be thinking about pursuing. Creating meaningful conversations can provide you with the wisdom you need to move forward.

We also tend to identify others as wisdom keepers while ignoring the wisdom within ourselves. Within each of us is a wise woman who knows what is best for us, and yet the voice of the wise woman can be silenced. Our life experiences can layer detritus over the very essence of who we are, and in our busyness we forget her. That wise woman lies buried in the place deep within ourselves, yet she is worth unearthing. Her voice offers us the gifts to move forward.

From a place of total misalignment and despair I started interviewing women, using the questions listed in Appendix 1. I discovered that:

1. **No matter who they were, each of these women had experienced a time in which they felt different, like they did not belong.** They felt different due to their skin colour, the fact that they were

introverted or extroverted, their size, their shape, the fact that they had to wear a uniform to school or they had terrible acne, how smart or not so smart they were perceived as by others and how that made them feel. They felt different because they spoke a different language at home or they came from a different country or nobody bothered to learn to pronounce their name properly.

2. **They had each struggled in their lives, and at times the struggle was instrumental in defining who they became.** The struggle was different, but the effects were the same: a push to reconcile something that limited their possibilities in order to move forward. They struggled with physical and sexual abuse, sexual identity, a parent in jail, cultural oppression, the death of a loved one, the addiction or mental illness of a loved one, or the beliefs of their family and culture.

3. **Most described their young childhood as magical.** For some it was about experiences with nature; others felt a sense of community, belonging, and adventure with their siblings and friends; others felt deep love from their parents, grandparents, aunties, or culture of origin; others felt belonging from the magical worlds they created in their own imaginations.

4. **At the age of seventeen, they did not all know what they wanted to be for the rest of their lives.** For most of the women I interviewed, life has not been a straight line. The route they took was winding, with some dead ends and rerouting. They each experimented with things to see how they fit. When things weren't a good fit, they went in another direction. They had moments of self-doubt and they stumbled. But the key is that they got back up again to experiment some more.

5. **They had a very personal way of defining success, and it was not just about money.** These women have a sense of purpose. They want to effect change in the world, and to do that they have

taken risks. They have felt heartache at times, yet they are passionate about what they do and the effect they want to have, so they continue.

Most of all, I discovered that in interviewing these women I felt fully alive, energized, and connected. I felt like myself again.

As I read and reread these women's words, I fell deeper in love with the women who shared so much of themselves with me. Their stories gave me the courage to finally leave the job I had clung to for so long for all the wrong reasons. I wanted to devote time to writing so I could share their wisdom with all of you. Over time, I was able to dive more deeply into how their stories could support me through my ever-evolving process of becoming. After leaving my job, I was in the process of becoming—becoming what, I wasn't sure, and yet I felt a sense of knowing, even under all my anxiety and loss, that I was making the right decision and everything would be all right. We are born with this potential within us, and our task is to evolve into the fullness of that potential. I truly believe that when we are able to show up as the full expression of ourselves, the world will be a better place.

From the stories of these exceptional women, I discovered an expansive formula, one that allows you to continually become the next level of yourself.

My first interview was with artist and entrepreneur Laüra Hollick. Laüra described her life as an upward spiral of being and becoming, of creating and re-creating herself. I was in awe of this description, especially from my place of imploding. I'd had tastes of that upward spiral in life, and I wanted to understand how to create and maintain it. When I asked Laüra if she ever gets in her own way, she said, "I am my own way. So in a sense I'm always in my way, but I don't view myself as an obstacle. I view myself as an ecosystem with many parts ultimately wanting to work together. Even when something appears as a boulder or obstacle within my own psyche, I accept it and include it in this ecosystem. I don't fight myself."

Laüra spoke my language when she used the word ecosystem to describe herself. It applied the message I had delivered during that meditation to us as individuals, to me as a woman. As a biologist, I understand what it means to be an ecosystem, and I grasped just how much energy I used fighting parts of myself that I labelled "bad," "wrong," or "not good enough." To actually welcome all of that and let go of the conflict within myself seemed like heaven—and the very definition of a thriving life.

My next interview was with Indigenous youth adviser Laura Kooji. She described how sometimes she got stuck in a downward vortex and her ex-husband was good at pulling her out of it. *Ah, a downward vortex;* that is exactly how I was feeling every morning as I drove to work.

So in my first two interviews I discovered these opposing forces: the upward spiral I was longing for and the downward vortex I felt stuck in. As I recalibrated my life after quitting my job, I knew I had to step out of one before I could enter the upward flow of the other. I needed to discover how to step out of the vortex for myself, but each of the other women I spoke with offered steps in this upward spiralling process. I talked to extraordinary women, from artists to politicians to educators and entrepreneurs. I have to thank Sheena Repath, co-founder and chief inspirer of making sh*t happen at MSH District, for opening her network to me. Without her, I would not have connected with these passionate entrepreneurs: Lisa Belanger, Devon Fiddler, Gloria Roheim McRae, Jocelyn Mercer, Janet Nezon, Nickolette Reid, and Jody Steinhauer. I was always surprised by how openly each woman shared her story and how excited they were by the idea of this book. I am forever grateful for the wisdom their life lessons gifted to me.

Each woman's story revealed that spiral of being and becoming, of creating and re-creating ourselves that Laüra had described. In order to live a whole, thriving life, it's necessary to let go of the conflict within ourselves, to accept ourselves as we are, and fully express that in the world. We are each in the driver's seat of our lives. I invite you to grab the wheel and take responsibility for what happens along the way. Understand who you are and what's important to you. Celebrate what makes you, you; don't hide it away. Have a purpose that is bigger than yourself. Know what drives you and the principles you want to live by. Take chances and try things out. If you feel compelled to do something, go out and give it a try; it will no doubt inform your next step.

Check in with yourself and ask, *Is this what I want, or is this something someone else has suggested I am supposed to do?* Let go of the supposed-to's that your culture, family, friends, school, or anyone else has imposed on you. *The only supposed-to you need is to be yourself.* Your journey is to find you, grow you, and celebrate you. Be compassionate with yourself and connect with people who are role models, who inspire you to be more of you. Remove the barriers that limit you from taking bold steps along the way, and always remember to nurture yourself. Sometimes a retreat or timeout (even a weekend off) is exactly what is needed to thrive.

I wrote this book for women (and men too) of all ages who are struggling with what to do with their lives, feeling listless, battling with "there must be something more," and questioning if they are capable enough, young enough, old enough, experienced enough, motivated enough, or courageous enough to make a change.

How to Use This Book

You aren't alone. You can change your life, let go of what holds you back, and become who you have always longed to be. These stories provide a path to do just that.

Mary Catherine Bateson, an American writer and anthropologist, said, "The human species thinks in metaphors and learns through stories." Stories provide us a structure to make sense of the world. Stories are powerful tools for creating change. Storytelling can build a sense of community and connection. When we hear what and how people have made things possible for themselves, we can learn and perhaps see what is possible for ourselves. How we interpret and make meaning of the stories we hear is personal. Our meaning-making is informed by who we are, how we were raised, and what our beliefs are. Stories can have layers of meanings, and sometimes those meanings can be contradictory.

As I read and reread the stories these women shared with me, I developed a deeper understanding. I was then able to apply their wisdom in different ways, adapting it as I change and grow. The lessons I received from these stories may be quite different from the lessons you receive. Consider the lessons I have learned and make sure you don't discount your own. Life is about discovering your own way forward and finding what brings you joy.

Notice whose story resonates with you, whose story doesn't speak to you, and whose story triggers strong emotions. Start to explore your reactions. What belief or way of thinking is causing you to react in that way? Is the story you have been telling yourself actually true? How can you begin to question your own narrative? Start to really explore and question yourself, your thoughts, behaviours, and beliefs. Getting curious about yourself is key to untangling your true nature and inhabiting your life. Knowing yourself and understanding what holds you back is an essential path to being and becoming.

Always remember: *You know what is best for you.* Think of this book as an offering of thoughts, ideas, inspirations, and stories that can nourish you on your journey. The stories and questions for self-reflection will nurture you, feed your growth, and allow you to move forward (even a little) in your life. Select what calls you, or what you are crying out for, and move toward it.

Although this book is only one step of your journey, I hope that you finish it by dreaming yourself into your next becoming: taking action for what really matters and making a difference in the world.

> 66 *I think that women are the heart and soul of humanity.* 99

JENNIFER GARBIN

2

IN HER OWN WORDS

Life Is an Upward Spiral of Being and Becoming

LAÜRA HOLLICK

Creative Spiritual Entrepreneur,
Artist, and Soul Art® Shaman

66 *What is most important to your spirit now?* **99**

I HAVE KNOWN LAÜRA Hollick for many years. I watched her transform from a timid, young artist barely making ends meet to a woman who ignites people globally with her creative heart. When I was thinking about who I wanted to interview, Laüra came to mind immediately. She seemed to be a master of dreaming the world, using her art and creativity to manifest a nü world. Laüra has been an extremely important part of my journey. I attended her Soul Art® workshops for years both in person and online. She has a knack for taking people deeply into themselves and spurring creativity from the soul. The paintings and doodles I have created over the years with Laüra have acted as sacred guideposts. I knew she would have wise words to share and I was eager to hear them.

Soul Art® Shaman Laüra Hollick is an award-winning artist, creative spiritual entrepreneur, and lover of the earth. For ten years, she hosted and produced a radio show on 93.3 FM CFMU called *The Artist's Lifestyle*, where she interviewed artists from all over the world about their lives, their work, and their creative process. In 2014, Laüra gave a TEDx Talk titled *You Are the Art,* where she encourages all of us to become creators. She was also the focus of a Bravo TV documentary, *The Artist's Life: Laüra Hollick.*

Through her Pure Inspiration newsletter and global events such as International Soul Art® Day and the *nü Icon Movie* (an annual guided vision quest to discover your iconic essence), Laüra's visionary art and insights inspire audiences around the world.

Laüra is the creator of Soul Art®, which is a unique creative practice that awakens our innate healing abilities, unleashes our creative genius, and taps into our intuition superpowers. She believes that each person's life is his or her soul's art, and she approaches her own life as living, breathing art.

Laüra's soul called on her to be an artist. But that meant letting go of the proverbial belief in the "starving artist" and building a successful business based on creating herself. Once Laüra let go of her limiting belief, her life began to change. Over the years, she has transformed herself time and time again. She used to timidly take small steps out of her comfort zone. Today, she makes big leaps into new expressions of herself and facilitates others to do the same. Laüra refers to this journey as "a cycle of being and becoming." In order to achieve that constant cycle of creating and re-creating herself, Laüra engages in continual self-exploration and lets go of old and sometimes unconscious beliefs. Laüra's story will guide you to create yourself from a place of wholeness and move forward through your own cycle of being and becoming.

Key messages from Laüra:

- Life is meant to be lived as a spiral of being and becoming, creating and re-creating yourself.
- Embrace the magic of your imagination to create your next becoming.
- Clear the beliefs keeping you isolated and separate by questioning the thought process holding the belief in place.
- Use your dream as a guide and inspiration to move forward.
- Re-evaluate and clarify to keep moving forward on your path.
- View yourself as an ecosystem, accepting yourself as whole and growing rather than as broken and needing fixing.
- Believe in yourself as the seed of your own success.

═══════════

I AM AN artist, a shaman, a creative and spiritual entrepreneur, and a lover of nature. I am dreaming a world lush with life. A pulse of magic courses through the veins of wind and water streams. There is a vibrant glow in the forest as the ecosystem sings with wisdom. I dream of a world where I can connect with nature.

My story is a journey of being and becoming. I am always in awe of the magic I experience in the moment while simultaneously seeking to evolve into my next expression. I have spiralled through this same experience of being and becoming again and again, with different stories dressing the underlying pattern. Every turning point in my life, every shift to the next level, has come from the acceptance and merging of being and becoming. As I accept where I am and continue to dream into who I want to be, I experience a turning point.

These are my tools for dreaming: art, Soul Art®, hiking in nature, journalling, creating guided journeys for others, leading by example, creative photo shoots, dancing, imagining, Pinterest, business, marketing, branding, and entrepreneurship. Soul Art® is a sacred journey of discovering and embodying your unique creative spiritual expression. Soul Art® is a process I developed that calls people from around the world to feel the one unifying desire we all have: the desire to tap into our own creative spiritual expression and let it become our sacred gift to the world.

When I was ten years old, my family moved to a place where an artist was living in the back of our home. I had never met an artist before and I was instantly intrigued. I used to go to her home and watch her create in her studio. I was invigorated by this experience and I looked forward to seeing her every day. As a young girl, I instantly recognized her creative essence and I loved to luxuriate in it. As a result, I activated my own creative essence. By recognizing her, I was able to recognize myself.

When I was young, I was deeply introspective and I struggled to connect. I spent most of my time imagining and dreaming of magical worlds I wanted to live in. I always felt deeply nourished in my own imaginary space. It was my home as a child. Growing up, there were two realities: my inner world (imagination and thoughts) of inspiration and magic and my outer world (the physical world) of confusion and disconnect. As an introvert more comfortable in my own imagination, I felt different, like I didn't quite fit in. As I've grown into adulthood, I've merged these two worlds and healed fears that kept the outer world looking so scary.

In order to create the life and career of my dreams, I was compelled to overcome my limiting beliefs about who I could be and what was possible for me financially. I was confused by the notion of making a living as an artist and I didn't quite know how to do it. On the path of inventing my own career and innovating ways to create my own money, I overcame tremendous survival and failure fears, as well as a sense of isolation. Although it was incredibly challenging at the time, I had such a strong vision of who I wanted to be that I always had the energy and desire to keep going. I believe it was my whole-hearted commitment that enabled me to cross the bridge from where I was to where I am now.

When things aren't working for me, I re-evaluate and clarify what is "off." Once I have clarified what has moved me off track, I swiftly return to what inspires me. It is a very natural and easy process for me to be in a perpetual state of inspiration; being inspired is my baseline. Even when something seems off, I can view it from the perspective of inspiration and understand its teaching. Allowing myself a lot of time and space for deep contemplation supports me to be in an inspired state most of the time. I know I'm on the right track when my spirit lights up from within and I feel a thriving ease. There may be challenges, or it may be smooth sailing, but when there is a wholehearted sense of "yes" within my being, I'm there.

Have I ever got in my own way? Hmm. I am my own way. In this sense, I'm always in my way, but I don't view myself as an obstacle. I view myself as an ecosystem, with many parts ultimately wanting to work together. Even when something appears as a boulder or obstacle within my own psyche, I accept it and include it in this ecosystem. I don't fight myself. I seek to accept and flow with all the moving parts of me. Of course, I have moments when I get caught up in something and I forget the bigger picture, but this is usually short-lived.

The best advice for living a successful life is to get to know yourself. You are your own greatest asset. Any success you experience will grow from your own core essence, so start watering the garden of your spirit and success will naturally sprout in your life.

AS A RESULT of Laüra's words, I am letting go of fighting myself. I see myself as an ecosystem and embrace my wholeness. Accepting "what is" seems to be the first step to creating my life as an upward spiral.

Questions for Self-Reflection

1. Laüra knows she's on track when her spirits light up from within and she feels a thriving ease. What lights you up? Make a list.

2. Laüra views herself as an ecosystem, with many parts working together. How would you describe the ecosystem you are today (a young forest, a desert, a raging river)? Channel your creative spirit and create a representation of your ecosystem in art, music, or words.

3. Even when something appears as an obstacle within her own psyche, Laüra accepts it and includes it in her ecosystem. What part of you or your experience are you not welcoming into your ecosystem? This could be a body part, a physical or personality characteristic, or a painful experience from the past. No matter what it is or was, welcome it as part of who you are and part of what you need to create yourself as a thriving ecosystem.

4. Laüra's belief that artists are supposed to be broke and hungry limited her success. What supposed-to are you believing that limits you? Dig deep: sometimes our beliefs about how we are supposed to be in the world can be well hidden.

5. Laüra feels most herself when she is creating art. When do you feel most yourself?

6. Laüra enters the upward spiral of being and becoming, of creating and re-creating herself by using art, creating herself as art. What do you use to create yourself? What could you use? (Hint: Take a look at what you wrote in the previous question.)

Dream as a Caretaker of the Planet

EVELYN ENCALADA GREZ

University Lecturer, Social Justice Activist,
and Multifaceted Soul

66 Dream as a caretaker of the planet. 99

I WAS INTRODUCED TO Evelyn Encalada Grez by a mutual friend who sent an email that read: "I am sometimes guided to connect people. Although you do not know each other, I believe you should." Very quickly I received an email from Evelyn: "Let's talk." We met in a busy, noisy coffee shop, and I was instantly captivated by the quiet mystery of Evelyn and the richness of her story.

Evelyn is an adjunct university professor, community organizer, and researcher. She lectures at UBC's Centre for Intercultural Communications and York University. Evelyn's doctoral studies had her splitting her time between Ontario and Mexico. Her dissertation is titled *Mexican Women Organizing Love, Life and Work: Transnational Storytelling from Rural Mexico and Canada*. She instills spirituality into her work and life as a practice of "transformation from the spirit within and the world throughout." Her teachings embody and mobilize knowledge for action and change. It is not enough to know—you must feel, act, and be transformed in the process.

Born in Chile and raised in Canada, Evelyn has lived in El Salvador, Nicaragua, Guatemala, and Honduras (working with the

Central American Network in Solidarity with Women Factory Workers), as well as Puebla, Mexico (working with El Centro de Apoyo al Trabajador/The Workers Support Centre).

Evelyn is a founding member of Justice for Migrant Workers, an award-winning political collective that has promoted migrant farm worker rights in Canada since 2001. She worked with film-maker Min Sook Lee on the critically acclaimed *El Contrato* (*The Contract*) and *Migrant Dreams*. Evelyn helps migrant farm workers create spaces to articulate their needs and dreams in their own voices, tell their own stories, and lead their own transnational human rights movement. In 2016, Evelyn was awarded the distinction of the most influential Latin American-Canadians by the Spanish-language newspaper *Correo Canadiense* for her academic and community work.

Evelyn has an intensity that demonstrates purposefulness. She also has an unquenchable desire to create connection. Her journey to belong drives her forward in her work to support migrant farm workers across Southern Ontario. Evelyn is deeply spiritual, gaining strength from her Chilean ancestry, her Christian upbringing, and Indigenous cultures around the globe. Her letting-go of how she was supposed to fit into Canada allowed her to find a sense of belonging with a community of people living between two worlds. Her power comes from living in the world between cultures, where everyone feels seen and recognized for who they are. From that place of understanding, a new sense of community is created, a community of unparalleled connections bound together by stories.

Key messages from Evelyn:

- Dream as if you are a caretaker of this planet.
- Connect, nurture community, and inspire others to dream.
- Sometimes your purpose chooses you.
- Our role is being part of the change whether we see the benefit in our lifetime or not.
- Enter the space of possibilities by embracing the uncomfortableness of stepping into something new for yourself.
- Being seen and recognized is powerful.
- Believe in something bigger than yourself.

———

AS AN ORGANIZER, much of what I do enlivens, instigates, and gives form to dreams. Organizers are dream keepers. Our actions are guided by dreaming possibilities, and this is how revolutionary movements and social movements have persisted throughout history. One of my dreams is that we live in a world without any borders. I may not see that goal being realized in my lifetime, but I want to be part of that historical process of change. I can't live in a world without being part of change. If I am not part of change, then I am just taking up air. My purpose is to effect change whether I benefit from it in the immediate- or the long-term; it does not matter. I have to be engaged in it. I inspire my students to dream. I teach my students about the boxes that society has encased us in, so they are cognizant.

I came from countries where many fought for a better world. They risked it all. They were the ones who dared to dream and they paid a huge price. They were tortured and killed for dreaming a different world, and they have been my main inspiration in life. I have felt the pain of the injustices of this world within my heart, my body, and my spirit. This compels me to dream because I know we can do better as human beings. By being engaged in dreaming a better world and by inspiring others to dream, I can remain true to my background—to my ancestors.

When I am on the farms working with the migrant worker community, I am in a different world. I am in a world that is so surreal. There is a lot of magical realism. People believe in other dimensions, not just the ones we see before our eyes. We are creating community in our own way. We are coming together across ethno-racial and linguistic lines and letting go of the debilitating divisions that exist among us. Migrant workers are in a third space—the space of possibilities. They are not completely bound to their country of origin, and in Canada they are treated like they don't belong. It is in that third space that we are able to negotiate ways of relating to one another where we strengthen one another to build community.

In the third space, there is a lot of pain because we all want to feel like we belong. But in this space, there are also so many other possibilities where we can detach ourselves and reinvent ways to see ourselves, and therefore reinvent ways to relate to one another. This is the space where I feel most comfortable. It is a space that deviates from duality, or from binaries.

My first turning point occurred before I was born. There was a military coup against the democratically elected socialist government in Chile, which of course set my destiny. I remember having a really beautiful childhood in Chile. Then my dad was forced to leave. My hair started falling out. I couldn't sleep properly. That is another reason I do the work that I do. I consider the children left behind and everything they go through. My mother and I followed my dad to Canada when I was five years old.

Being uprooted from one's country is very painful. As a child, you basically have no voice, no choice, you are just taken. I was also uprooted from my grandparents. I lost my second mother. In plenty of countries we all live together, multiple generations in one space. A disconnection exists in Canada that is so foreign to many people. I felt like when I came to Canada, the light within me went out. Throughout my life, I have tried to turn this light back on and make it shine as bright as possible.

I faced a lot of discrimination when I was growing up because I was the only Latin American student in my school and did not know the language. It was awful. I was called horrible names. Other children were completely unforgiving. There is a lot of bullying in schools, and if you don't speak English and you look different, then you are definitely going to be a target. So I had to contend with that. Schooling was a reflection of the rest of Canada, and Canada wanted to socialize me and mould me. I always found school and the schooling system, the socialization of schooling, to be very violent. It was difficult to feel connected when I had one world at home—where Chile still existed but quite statically—and then was thrust into the rest of Canada by myself and not able to defend myself. Throughout my young life, my parents instilled working-class values in me. My parents were very radical, and I started to question everything they were teaching me. You know, are these values being imposed upon me? Are these values really mine?

In 2001, I got a phone call from a friend. The United Farm Workers of America needed a translator on an investigative mission. Apparently, twenty-one migrant farm workers from Mexico were deported for organizing a labour stoppage near Leamington, Ontario. A group of activists was travelling there to understand exactly what had taken place. It was a very surreal weekend. We went to all the places where migrant workers hung out. I nearly lost my voice because I talked to so many people. The workers felt like machines. As machines, they were not allowed to break down, get sick, or get injured without losing their jobs, losing their work permits, and being sent home. Their work was arduous and dangerous. When I heard about everything they were going through, I saw everything. I had tried to escape all of my differences and my journey to finally feel I belonged in Canada. All of this crumbled. I realized that if people who looked like me were being treated this way, then I haven't made it—nobody has made it. I couldn't just say, "So thanks for coming out and speaking to me. See you later." I have since dedicated my life to working with the migrant worker population.

When I was researching for my PhD, I lived in Mexico. A year after I came back to Canada, I was questioning my work. I was exhausted. One night I had a nervous breakdown. I was drained, I couldn't sleep. I prayed to the angels, to God, to anyone out there listening: *Please, please, please send me a sign. Show me if I am throwing my life away. Show me if I am to continue on this journey. Show me if I am living my true purpose.* I prayed really hard, with all my heart and soul, and I finally fell asleep. In the morning, I checked my email, and there in my inbox was an invitation to the United Nations. An all-expenses-paid chance to talk about my community work with the migrant worker population, specifically women, to commemorate the first-ever International Rural Women's Day. If that's not a sign, I don't know what is. I went to the UN and gave a heartfelt speech.

I don't even try to leave anymore because the migrant workers are my community. They witness me, and I witness them. I am part of this journey and I have to continue walking with them because we "see" each other. They recognize me. They pull me back in. Witnessing, to me, means being present, trustworthy, listening, and reminding people of all the beautiful traits they have within. Not taking away their power but reminding them they already have the strength. They are already doing it.

When things aren't working for me, I retreat. This week I definitely needed to retreat because I was becoming too overwhelmed with too many cases and so many issues. So I'm in retreat mode. In that way, I can get my energy back, collect my energy wherever else I left it. I go back to my healers, my women healers. A lot of times they can be channels to Spirit when I am too clouded to hear messages. I can be more clear to hear the messages I need. So I definitely need them in my life. We have to take care of ourselves in this work because when we care for ourselves, we can really be there for other people. If we are not there for ourselves, then we will fall apart. We'll get sick.

Taking care of ourselves is as much about taking care of others as it is about ourselves. It's necessary for us; it's about being more of a light in this world. Of course, we have all this light and darkness within us, but we all have the responsibility to send out positive energy in the world. If I'm feeling really tired, then I feel like I do have to retreat in order to recollect my thoughts, get my energy back, and then ask Spirit, *What is my purpose?* and to send me signs. That is when new things start to unfold. We can all use a retreat, a sabbatical from ourselves and from the rest of the world in order to keep us doing what we are meant to do. I don't think I could do this work without taking little retreats. That way I can go back into the community and be stronger than before.

I may not be rich with money, but I am rich in other ways. I have that type of recognition being mirrored back to me. I try to mirror back a lot of strength and humanity to all the workers—all the people I work with. Then I realize that is all part of our community work—really recognizing one another, really seeing one another. I am there to be a mirror and then a bridge sometimes, or a connector to other resources.

I know I'm on the right track because of the way that I feel— coherent. I'm feeling coherent with my values, and things are just evolving with me. Things are just laying themselves out before me. Things just flow. When I am in that space, more positive things happen.

When I deviate from my path, there is more heartache. It's almost like the universe communicates to me that I have to get back on track and get out of my own way sometimes. I know I'm on the right track too when I'm feeling tired but then go out and do community work or teach and it gives me all this energy I had no idea I had. It is energy that just comes naturally to me and time flies; work doesn't feel like work because I am totally in the moment. We hear about the power of now, but to experience that power is something else. It's contemplative. It is empowering, so beautiful. That's when you know you are doing exactly what you came here to do in the world.

———

THROUGH EVELYN'S STORY, I realize that I have always dreamed as a caretaker of the planet. My dream for the planet has always been that we see ourselves as nature. The way I apply that dream is slightly different now. My dream is for a mind shift from surviving to thriving, from fear to love and acceptance, from a sense of feeling separate to one of belonging.

Questions for Self-Reflection

1. Evelyn wants to live in a world without borders and is making herself part of that historical change. What historical change do you want to be part of?

2. Evelyn sees her work as an organizer as enlivening, instigating, and giving form to dreams. How do you enliven, instigate, and give form to your dreams and the dreams of others?

3. Evelyn continues her work with the migrant workers because they witness her, they are present with her, they listen, they remind

her of her beautiful traits. Who witnesses you? Who reminds you of your beautiful traits? Who witnessed you in the past? How did that make you feel? How do you witness yourself now?

4. Now look for opportunities where you can recognize other people. Who do you recognize? Who do you actively remind of their beautiful traits? Who could you recognize? Make a list of those people. What are their beautiful traits?

5. Now write them a note, an email, tell them in person what beautiful things you see in them and what a wonderful effect they have had on your life.

6. Make recognizing other people a part of your daily practice. Notice what effect it has on you.

The Power
of Diversity

JENNIFER GARBIN

Pastor, Mother, and Wife

> 66 *I surround myself with people who dream big dreams.* 99

I MET JENNIFER GARBIN when I was facilitating an Open Space event in Guelph, Ontario. She had closely cropped hair and an energy about her that exuded joy, acceptance, and love. I had no idea what she did for a living, but there was something intriguing about her that made me want to know more.

Jennifer is eclectic. She has owned her own businesses, including freelance graphic design, photography, wedding cake baking, and flower arranging. It took her sixteen years to complete her undergraduate degree before she went on to receive her master of divinity from Emmanuel College, University of Toronto. Jennifer is a lifelong learner and has gone on to pursue her doctorate of ministry, which explores how emerging young Canadian Christian adults who don't attend public worship are living out their faith and reimaging what Church means. Jennifer loves research and has a passion for anti-poverty activism and sustainable living. She believes that when safe spaces are created for real dialogue and people are given permission to explore and ask questions about scripture and their shared experience, amazing things happen. Jennifer is an avid painter and gardener. She loves to grow green edible things in her backyard as part of her commitment to sustainable living.

Jennifer's interest in her community is palpable. She is not my typical idea of a faith leader. I am exposing my biases and beliefs when I say that. When I think of a faith leader, I think of a conservative, middle-aged man with a collar and robes. It was refreshing to see this vibrant woman with an interest not only in her church but also in the broader community of Guelph. She speaks passionately about how we hold the seed to our own happiness: it starts with loving yourself. Jennifer has tried many things in life and has repeatedly let go of long-held beliefs. Hearing the words "God uses all kinds of people for all kinds of things" opened possibilities for Jennifer. She recognizes how her perspectives shifted as she exposed herself to diversity and learned about herself. Jennifer's lessons are about the power that comes from meeting and understanding the "other." She defines the "other" as the people whom we judge as different and separate from ourselves because of the beliefs we hold about them.

Key messages from Jennifer:

- Recognize that you are the seed of your own happiness.
- Words are powerful. Be careful what you ask for.
- The world is not black and white.
- Take the time it takes. It is okay to take longer to finish the job.
- Expose yourself to diversity—it shifts perspectives and creates understanding.
- Whenever we encounter the "other," there is an opportunity to learn about ourselves.

MY DREAM FOR the world is that people realize that within themselves lies the seed of their own happiness, success, and peace. Put simply, I learn to love myself and say, *Hey, you know, I do have gifts. I do have skills. I am a lovable person even though I don't feel like it sometimes.* So as a loveable person, my task is to love others. That's a dream I have. We don't really recognize our capacity for loving because we do not see ourselves as being loveable creatures. When we put aside the fear of others, the fear of our own inadequacy, and recognize that we are enough, when we begin to love ourselves as human beings, then that fear of loving others drops away. When we realize that it is within us, that we have the power to change not only ourselves but also the world around us. Then all of a sudden we stop blaming everybody else. Hate stops. Fear stops. The opposite of fear is love. It is when we realize that we are not controlled by fear that we allow ourselves to risk loving.

As a pastor, dreaming of the potential of humanity is huge. It is central to everything we do. We are living in a world that we believe can be better, where humans attend to one another—a world full of love. The key is to be engaged in things that feed us and also feed others. Frederick Buechner [an American writer and theologian] once said, "The place that God calls you to is the place where your deep gladness and the world's deep hunger meet."

It is so important to put out into the universe the idea that "this is what I wish I was." If we put that out into the universe, the universe conspires with us to make those things happen. When we say things like, "I wish I was" or "One day I will be," there is an intention there. It means we have to be quite careful with the words we use, with what we ask for. I learned a long time ago not to pray for patience because what happens afterwards really sucks. So often we go through life not being intentional.

So, a funny example from my last year of high school. In my locker, I posted a page from a magazine of two Italian sports cars that read: "A passion for Italian bodies." I wasn't a car buff. I just thought it was really funny. When it came to yearbook time, they asked for my catchphrase and I said, "Ugh. I can't stand this stuff." What I put down was, "A passion for Italian bodies." I didn't care. What is really, really, really ironic is that I met and married a guy who is Italian.

The folks who have influenced my life and the people I surround myself with are people who dream big dreams. It is important to sometimes have those "pie in the sky" thoughts where you think, *I wonder if someday...* I surround myself with people who ask good questions.

My perspective has changed several times in my life. When I was in my mid-teens, I had a sense I was going to be a pastor. I really had this conviction that one day I would lead a church. I grew up in a denomination where women were not allowed to speak. We all had long hair and there were no women elders or leaders in our church. Women were not allowed to serve in any kind of way. It was very, very restrictive. So I am sitting there going, *Oh my goodness, I am feeling a call from God to be a pastor, but how can I do that when the Bible says I am not allowed?* When I was with the Baptist

Church, I had a conversation with my pastor and I asked him what I should do. His comment to me was: "God uses all kinds of people for all kinds of things." It was the first time I heard anyone say, "You know what, keep dreaming. There is space for this." It was the first time I realized maybe the world isn't black and white. There is more than one way to look at things.

It took me sixteen years to finish my bachelor of arts degree, but I got it done. I got married, had kids, and worked all over the world. At one point, I worked as a freelance graphic designer with a lesbian couple. They were really good friends of mine. The new law in Ontario allowed same-sex marriage just as I was leaving to pursue my master of divinity degree. Just before I left for school, we went for lunch and they said to me, "You know, this is great. This is fantastic. The law has changed and we are so proud of you. You are going to become a pastor and when you are done, you can marry us." I thought, *Oh my goodness, what do I do?* I mean, I loved them. They were fantastic, but marriage was between a man and a woman. This is how I had been raised. I was really conflicted about it, so I made up some excuse about how I was probably going to be stationed in Nova Scotia, where I was eventually stationed. This goes to show that you have to be careful about what you say because the universe conspires to make it happen. So I joked about it, poo-pooed it, and went off to seminary.

At the United Church of Canada Seminary, many folks there were from the LGBTQ community who had been cast out of their own denominations because of their sexuality. So I worked, talked, and studied with LGBTQ folks all the time. What I realized in these conversations was that they are just as faithful and just as wonderful, even more so sometimes, than any straight person I had ever known. They are just as called by God.

All of a sudden it came back to me: my sixteen-year-old self sitting with my pastor, who was saying, "God uses all kinds of people for all kinds of things." At that moment, I realized, *Oh my goodness, this is not about what I believe, it is about something bigger. This is about justice. This is about equity, about wholeness, about being whole in the world, being loved.* That was a huge turning point for me. And you know, the first wedding I did when I graduated was my two lesbian friends. This was a huge eye-opener for me. Whenever we encounter the "other," we learn so much about ourselves. So here I was, this person raised in a Christian home, taught by my religion to be a homophobe, being met with love and acceptance and grace.

I now realize that every person I encounter has this same potential for transformation. It is through sitting, learning, and listening to who they are—their story—and being able to be a witness to their story, that is a truly humbling experience. There is always a moment when not only am I learning about them, I am learning about myself. I'm learning about humanity and I am learning about what this world could be like if there were moments where hearts were able to touch hearts.

I believe that the will of the universe is that we all be one, that we be together, that we be in relationship. We need to be in relationship with one another. To be a human being is to be in relationship. You wouldn't have survived, you wouldn't have been born without relationship. So when we are working toward these things, not for our own good, but for the good of each other, not to the total exclusion of self, but being engaged in mutual relationships, there is a total knowingness that says, "Yeah, this is right."

———————

JENNIFER REMINDED ME of the power of words in manifesting our reality and that setting a clear intention helps to powerfully move us forward. I also learned from her that some things take time to create and that's okay. I am learning not to push but to relax and allow things to unfold.

Questions for Self-Reflection

1. Jennifer spoke of the power of intention, to clearly state this is what I wish I was. What is the intention you have for your life? For the world? For today? For this moment?

2. Her close friendship with the lesbian couple she worked with did not change Jennifer's strongly held beliefs about same-sex marriage. It wasn't until seminary where she met and built relationships with LGBTQ folks who had been cast out of their own denominations that she appreciated their faith and devotion. What has happened in your life to change your perspective?

3. In the church that Jennifer was raised in, women were considered the "other." Who do you see as the "other"? Be really honest with yourself here. Who do you judge for not being like you? Politicians, an ethnic group, or a person in your neighbourhood, school, workplace, or even your family who doesn't think like you, look like you, or act like you?

4. Jennifer used to believe that only men could be leaders in the church—a black-and-white belief. Where do you see the world as black and white, right and wrong, good and bad? What if it wasn't true? How can you allow space for more "grey" thinking?

5. Through the diversity of seminary, Jennifer had the revelation that acceptance is about equity, wholeness, and being loved. How could you open yourself to explore diversity and harvest the lessons it brings?

6. Jennifer surrounds herself with people who ask good questions. Who around you asks good questions? You know, the type of questions that make you really think about yourself, your community, your world; the ones that stretch your thinking and challenge your perspectives. What good questions could you ask those around you, to expand their thinking and perhaps create something together?

Getting to Alignment

LAURA KOOJI

Indigenous Youth Adviser

> *Dreaming is a powerful portal into our ancestry and into our future. What each of us knows is that which we have experienced. What matters is what we choose to do with each experience.*

I MET LAURA KOOJI in an online course. I knew very little about her, but I felt that she had some piece of the puzzle that was important for me to hear. We first met in person in a relaxed coffee shop that had the feel of a community hub. I waited for her, kept checking my watch, and finally called her. She had forgotten about the interview and ended up running over to meet me. I was so glad I waited. Laura and her guiding principles held an important key for me and for this book.

Laura is a social services worker with a passion for Indigenous justice. Her educational background is in visual and performing arts from Humber College and fitness and wellness leadership from Mohawk College. Working in social services, Laura felt that not having a university degree in social work or equivalent got in the way of her success. Then her decolonized mind kicked in and she acknowledged that her real education comes from the "University of the Universe" and her Anishinaabe roots. Her social services work has included supporting immigrant women and working with incarcerated women. At the same time, Laura has run a yoga, wellness, and movement coach business. As a youth adviser, Laura advocates for Indigenous students in the Ontario educational system and supports them in connecting with their cultural roots and with elders from their Nation(s). Laura also assists schoolteachers with including Indigenous teachings within the curriculum.

Laura's Anishinaabe values—the Seven Grandfather Teachings (see Appendix 2) and her community of aunties who taught her the Thirteen Grandmother Moon Teachings (see Appendix 3)—have helped her to stay grounded. Laura taught me that women have a very important role in Indigenous culture, not only in supporting one another but also in supporting and nurturing family, community, and the land. Women have a close connection to the cycles of the moon, and the Grandmother Moon Teachings are about honouring the cycle of the moon and the wisdom each of the thirteen moons offer (there are thirteen moons every year).

Laura let go of her relationship supposed-to so she could fully embrace her own sexuality. She also let go of the idea that she is supposed to have a university education to succeed as she embraced her Indigenous roots and decolonized her thinking. In his article "Decolonize Your Mind," Isaac Giron describes decolonization in this way: "A person with a decolonized mind accepts their past, loves their present and creates their future, regardless of what stands in their way."

Key messages from Laura:

- Your values can guide you through dark times.
- Consciously align your thoughts, words, and actions with your values.
- We all have struggles that create a feeling of separation.
- Surround yourself with people who remind you of your awesomeness.
- Find someone who reminds you of what you stand for.
- Love yourself even in times of darkness.
- Notice when you are being called to something new and act upon it.
- What we know is what we have experienced, read, and written.

———

MY VALUES COME from my Indigenous culture. The Grandmother and Grandfather Teachings are kind of like my Ten Commandments. When I look through those teachings, when I align with those values, I see and interpret the world and it ultimately becomes how I dream it. The Seven Grandfather Teachings are really the most simple, simple things—love, wisdom, truth, bravery, honesty, humility, and respect. So when I'm feeling frustrated with whatever is going on, I go back and ask myself, *Are my thoughts, words, and actions in alignment?* If I am not in alignment, then I focus on getting back because I know nothing will happen the way it is intended to if things aren't jiving. I have to do what is necessary to get aligned. If it is sitting down and writing a task list, then I do that. If it is going for a walk and clearing my head, then I do that.

To be in alignment for some people may mean ending a relationship. Leaving an unsupportive friend or family member is the hardest part of getting to alignment. It's difficult for people who don't have supportive relationships in their life to let go of a friend or relation they no longer align with. It's one thing when you are on your own and you can be in charge of your own destiny, but if you don't have somebody beside you who is supporting you, that can be a big problem. My ex-husband was really good at that. When I got into a funk, he just didn't put up with it. He was like, "Pull up your socks, get to work, stop making excuses, stop whining and complaining." His comments whipped me into shape and it was quite lovely. It was not always what I wanted to hear, but it was what I needed to get out of the "stuck" vortex.

There is a triangle, basically a vortex. There is a victim, there is a rescuer, and there is the oppressor. In that triangle, when we are feeling bad, we can find ourselves in any one of these situations and sometimes spend our entire lives rotating in this triangle, shifting from victim to rescuer to revenge [oppressor]. And you know, working in social services, I have seen that play out. What this does to people is unbelievable. Even in situations where people do have their core needs met. People are still running around with tons of money in their pockets and they are spending their lives in that energy. Feeding any one of those three things is not going to help you. When you think of ways where you try to save someone who is broken, or ways to seek out revenge against another person, or go internal as a victim and say, "Oh, poor me, why did the universe do this to me?" you are just feeding that vortex and you are not going to come out the other side of it. Instead, you will fall deeper and deeper into the vortex. My ex-husband wouldn't feed the vortex and he refused to go down it with me.

We shared seventeen years together. When we met, we had so much in common, but there was this dynamic of the older guy and the younger girl. I found him to be a refuge and a guide and that was a beautiful thing, but I outgrew it. Things started to fall apart. I decided to come out and live fully as Two Spirit. I'd been out to selective people as bisexual since I was sixteen, and for years my husband would say, "You're gay, just be gay." I had invested so much time and love. I was like, "No, no, no this is what you do. You stick it out. You fight the good fight. You keep going." We both evolved and we both changed and both in great and wonderful ways and yet there are ways that we are just not compatible anymore.

When I was really young, my life was very sweet. It was really all about creativity, imagination, and dreaming—prime of my inno- cence, really. When I turned twelve, I moved into the city. It was like saying goodbye to everything I knew. I was bullied severely for about two years in my new school. The damage that was done took me years to repair. The bullying pushed me into rebelling. After high school, I fell apart. I was done. My partying got out of hand, and the decisions I made put me in some risky situations. I was in a very misguided place trying to find the love I needed from myself in all the wrong places. That lasted for about two years.

I talk about walking in two worlds. As a Two Spirit person, I have walked the darkest road of one culture [mainstream society] and in the purest light of the other [Indigenous culture]. I know what it feels like to be an outsider. I never felt like I neatly belonged in any box. I never felt I belonged anywhere. So my teenage years were no picnic. They were harsh. Fortunately, I was blessed with support- ive parents, and I'm blessed to have that cultural piece that held me together. It saved my life having those early values and teach- ings. I always knew the path I was taking wasn't right for me, that I was just pushing my boundaries. I knew I was rebelling and I knew there was something better on the other side and that I would grow up and be okay. Fortunately, I had a soft place to land and so it taught me the value of what I learned from my moon lodge. I grew up with this beautiful lodge of women who were so support- ive. Girls go through a right-of-passage that involves a berry fast when we go through our first moon cycle [menstruation]. Then we enter the moon lodge for that year and receive our teachings from our aunties on how to take care of ourselves—the strawberry teachings. All of those really important lessons on self-care, self-love, taking care of our body, and being a woman supported me through the tough times. My mother would say, "You are better than that. You are better than thinking or feeling that way." So there was someone in the background saying, "You're awesome, don't forget that you are awesome," and that helps me to get through to the other side. I know what it's like to come out the other side of all that pain and go, "Holy smokes, I'm amazing!"

So I would say to others: through that darkness, just try to be loving toward yourself. If you give yourself the love you are trying to give others, no matter what you go through, you will always come out the other side stronger. You might experience a few horrible things—we can't control what happens to us or messages that the world may send us about how worthy of love we are. However, we can choose how we respond. We can create boundaries and standards around how we are treated by others. We can choose our core truth. Through love, we continually move toward the light.

At one point, I was working as an outreach worker helping with women in the prison system. I had this moment where I was sitting in a maximum-security prison. I was waiting to speak with a woman. For a moment, I witnessed myself. In that little witness moment, I asked myself, *What am I doing sitting in a maximum security prison? How did I get here?* It was a question that someone who had gotten themselves into prison would ask, and here I was asking myself, *How did I get here?* Although I was really there for just a few moments, as I looked back at my past I recognized that I was just a few bad decisions away from being in the inmate's position. Again, I had to ask myself, *Is this really what my spirit wants? Is this what I want to do?* So that was sort of my call to adventure, a sort of wake-up call, and I started to explore other paths.

I started Earth Moves, a social enterprise. My dream for Earth Moves was to bridge well-being across communities through active living. I empowered individuals and communities to support and learn about one another through wellness and economic innovation. I worked within the Indigenous communities and shifted my focus to dreaming a world that embraces the Indigenous worldview. I feel strongly about decolonizing the mind, body, and spirit because that shift will address sexism, homophobia, racism, poverty, the environment, peace, and everything. I think we have been really beaten to a pulp to feel that we have to constantly work to get more, and to measure up. We have to shift this mindset, as our children are dying because they feel small and insignificant.

I really had to decolonize my idea of education and wisdom, and I recognize that I earned my eagle feathers at a very young age. I see myself as a permanent student of the university of the universe. What each of us knows is what we have experienced, what we have read, what we have written. The only thing that matters is what we choose to do with it. What I had to overcome was my own sense of shortcoming. I did not go to university, so I didn't get a degree in something applicable to my field, like social work. Feeling like you are "enough" (good enough, smart enough, strong enough) is huge in our society.

I HAVE A great deal of gratitude to Laura for sharing her wisdom of the downward vortex. Understanding that it exists and clearly seeing how I was stuck in it for so long helped me to pull myself out. I recognize now that my favourite role is rescuer and playing that role exhausts me. What I have discovered is that it was not possible for me to enter the upward spiral until I had stepped out of my downward vortex and nurtured myself.

Questions for Self-Reflection

1. Laura clearly understands her guiding principles and knows how to apply the Grandmother and Grandfather Teachings to how she thinks, acts, and speaks. What values and principles guide you?

2. When Laura is feeling frustrated, when she is making excuses, whining and complaining, she goes back and asks herself, *Are my thoughts, feelings, and actions in alignment with the Grandmother and Grandfather Teachings?* What happens when you are misaligned? How do you feel physically, emotionally, and spiritually? How do you react?

3. Sitting in a maximum-security prison waiting to meet with a client, Laura asked herself, *How did I get here?* Have you ever had that kind of moment? She asked herself, *Is this what my spirit really wants me to do?* What does your spirit really want you to do?

4. Laura grew up with this beautiful lodge of women, her aunties, who were so supportive. Throughout her life, Laura's mother has been there to remind her of her awesomeness. Who reminds you of your awesomeness?

5. You can remind yourself of your awesomeness. When have you felt awesome? Make a list of those moments. What were you doing, who were you with, where were you? Write an "I'm awesome" letter to yourself to remind yourself just how awesome you are.

6. Pay attention to when people say nice things about you. Say thank you and just breathe it in. Let it really land for you. Then remind someone else just how awesome they are.

I Speak to the World Through Theatre

YASMINE KANDIL

Assistant Professor, Drama in Education
and Applied Theatre

> ❝ *I am the only person who can love me the way that I want to be loved.* ❞

I MET YASMINE KANDIL at a social justice conference at Brock University. I went to the conference in search of relationships that would support me intellectually, emotionally, and spiritually. I was feeling so disconnected at work that I needed to look elsewhere for the types of relationships I wanted in my life. I asked myself, *Where would I find those kinds of people?* The next thing I remember is coming face to face with a notice for the social justice conference and a light bulb went off: *That is where my people will be.* So I went. I really enjoyed the conference. It was quite thought-provoking. At lunch Yasmine and I connected and we have been friends ever since.

I am absolutely in love with what Yasmine does. She teaches applied theatre, which is such a powerful way to transform people's perspectives and create a depth of understanding that jumpstarts difficult conversations and moves people beyond their closely held views. Yasmine is originally from Egypt. She has a bachelor of arts in theatre from the University of Cairo, as well as a master of fine arts in theatre directing and a PhD in applied theatre, both from the University of Victoria. Her dance with applied theatre began with young garbage pickers in the slums of Cairo. In collaboration with Community Institutional Development, she created a theatre program run by those garbage pickers, focusing on the marginalization they experienced.

Yasmine is full of life. She identifies as a Middle Eastern woman who is fiercely faithful and loyal to Canada because Canada opened its doors to her in a way her country could not. She is a lover of all people. She thoroughly enjoys engaging with other people. It fuels her. She was doing what she loved without knowing what it was called. She pursued her academic studies in order to gain the skills she needed to teach others to direct their own pieces and to speak to the world through theatre. The arts are an afterthought and viewed mostly as entertainment in our society. The power and influence of the arts in transforming perspectives is overlooked by so many. Applied theatre unquestionably affects communities in which the work is done. Being an academic has given her the opportunity to feel the respect that the arts deserve, a feeling that was missing in her early career.

Key messages from Yasmine:

- You may already be doing what it is that brings you alive.
- Your family history, culture, and values allow you to approach change from a place of rootedness.
- You are the only one who can love you the way you want to be loved.
- Just sit with the hurt. Accept it as what is right now and see what opens up for you.
- Sometimes to fit in we may crush a part of ourselves.
- Bringing back your heritage and culture into the way you associate with yourself may be empowering.
- Celebrating your uniqueness is enriching.
- A great gift we can provide each other is space to express our uniqueness.

―――――

I WOULD LIKE to live in a world of engagement, respectful engagement. Where people celebrate culture and diversity, celebrate one another's values and learn from one another. Where people are humble enough to admit defeat and their own mistakes and where capitalism doesn't run our agenda and our lives. Where the emphasis on family and human connection is more apparent and more stressed than the emphasis on career and the drive to make more money and to acquire more. I genuinely believe that the work that I do with students and communities contributes to making the world a world that I would like to live in.

I gravitated toward movies when I was young. I enjoyed creating scenes, holding a camera and videoing things, manipulating what goes on in the camera frame. I wanted to pursue cinema studies at university, but the American University in Cairo didn't have film studies. I reluctantly went into theatre and just fell in love with it. The thorough discipline of understanding intricate moments within our lives and re-creating that through the theatre was such a heavenly place. I channel a lot of my energy in my theatre work. I think that I speak to the world through theatre. That is how I engage the world. I feel like theatre is air for me. If I don't do theatre, I don't think I'm alive.

I was doing applied theatre without knowing it was called applied theatre. I was simply using my theatre skills in working with the community because I needed the income. Somebody said, "We have a bunch of young garbage pickers, can you work with them?" I asked, "Can you pay me?" He said, "Yes." I said, "Sure." I worked with the kids for two years and fell in love with them. We created a performance that was innocent and beautiful and celebratory, and it gained a lot of acknowledgement from the NGO [non-governmental organization] that was funding the work. Everyone got excited and they wanted to do another performance.

The second performance was a little darker, naturally. Egypt was going through a very dark phase of Mubarak, the succession of his son, and there were more arrests happening and the Iraq War was going on and everybody's spirits were low. We channel that energy into creating our art. We might not necessarily speak directly about what is in our heart, but we reflect it. The performance had a much more cynical tone. It brought to life some of the less pleasant realities of their lives—prostitution, gambling, drugs—in a very comedic way. The NGO manager came and watched the performance and said we shouldn't be performing it because it would bring shame to the community. The performance went on anyway.

Afterwards, the funding dried up. So even though the experience of creating the theatre piece was empowering, the kids still rely on sources of funding by NGOs to provide facilitators like me. That is what prompted me to learn how to teach directing. I wanted to teach those kids the skills they needed to direct their own pieces.

That is how I ended up at the University of Victoria for my master's degree. It was there that I learned that what I was doing with the garbage pickers was called "applied theatre" and I went on to do my PhD in applied theatre.

I value Canada so much because it's embraced me. I was twenty-eight when I came to Canada, and as an Egyptian I was pretty solid in who I was. I was in a relationship with a Canadian who had kids and their own values. Negotiating that space with someone and trying to fit into that dynamic and still keep my faith and traditions was very hard. Part of the allure of faith and tradition is that it builds community.

The ways that I could build community in this relationship was through Thanksgiving, Christmas, family reunions, all of which I enjoyed. When I decided to bring back my own heritage and culture into the way that I associate with myself, I started to truly feel much more empowered. I had to reckon with *Who are you really?* and *What are the values that distinguish you from other people?* My values and the way I was raised, my Egyptian side, makes me a unique individual that I can celebrate personally, in the midst of all these wonderful Canadian people and their values. My parents and family history taught me to live my life with dignity and in moderation, to go out of my way to support others, and to speak up for those who are not able to speak up for themselves. We were taught to see life as a gift and to live each day like it is a gift. I think these things are very important to remember as an immigrant too, because when you leave your family behind you have to start from scratch. And sometimes it can be very unsettling to be in a new environment and not quite know people's values.

I worked with young immigrant and refugee teens, and I noticed that in their schools most of them are trying to become Canadian by looking and speaking and doing what Canadians do. And a lot of them feel a huge sense of loss inside their hearts. You can imagine as a teenager—you don't always know how to articulate it, but you feel like you have crushed something inside you and that is your personal heritage. It is embodied in the memories you have left behind when you left home. You are not allowed to miss that because there is not space for that in school, and school occupies most of your life.

There is an erasure of sorts and it is not perpetuated by someone in particular—it is just a societal thing. It is an inability to know how to genuinely integrate someone else's culture. There is a curiosity, almost a delight, in exoticizing the difference of the "other" rather than genuinely accepting that difference and integrating with it. It is nobody's fault. And so it is the immigrant person who has to say, What do I do with that? Because if you go with the flow and you get swept by the wave of becoming Canadian, there will be no room for the values that shaped you as a person, that make you unique. You have to bring those back because part of celebrating your new journey in Canada is celebrating the person who came to Canada.

In the Middle East, there is a lot of emphasis on human relations and family love. You expect people to drop by. You always have something sweet on the counter in case someone drops by. When people come by, they just hang out. There is no quick agenda. There is no quick visit and go. There is just hanging out. Sometimes people will come and they will just spend the night. So we have an extra little room in our house. When my mom's cousin visits, she just spends a couple of nights. And she lives in Cairo. I think the emphasis on family in the Middle East is so enriching. Family extends beyond the nuclear family to aunts, uncles, cousins, neighbours, and friends. It just becomes this big lovely festival, this carnival of relationships.

In the Middle East, if you meet someone today and become friends, you can expect a call from them tomorrow and the day after, and then we are calling each other every day and it doesn't fade out. You just acquire more and more friends. And those friends, not a single week goes by without that contact at least twice or three times a week. Contact that means phone calls, not just texts but actual phone calls and visits. It just becomes what life is. People have a bigger ability to trust others. When I came to North America, I felt the difference.

The biggest and most recent lesson I've had to learn is associated with my personal need in relationships. All my life, all I wanted was to be with someone who could love me. I thought if I could have that I would be the happiest woman on earth. I realized after my last relationship ended that I am the only person who can love me the way that I want to be loved. If I could give that to myself, I would be a very happy person. Then I will embark upon whatever happens in the future from that place of feeling fulfilled.

The lesson didn't come easily. When you lose someone you love, you don't know what to do with yourself. It is all-encompassing and you start to question why you were in the relationship, and the whole feeling of rejection is amplified. Then after a while you just sit with all that and you say, *Well, this is my situation right now and I have to accept it,* and it is when you accept it that you actually make peace with not having the dream that you thought you actually needed so much. That is when you start to love yourself, be kind to yourself, nurture yourself, and it is when you start to go through that process you learn that this is the biggest love you will ever need, the love of oneself. I don't mean that in a selfish way; I just mean it in a kind, thoughtful, compassionate way. If I can't love myself, how could I possibly expect me, as a whole person, to enjoy being with somebody else? I was with that other person seeking something I couldn't give to myself. So it couldn't have been healthy and it couldn't have been satisfying, no matter what.

If I hadn't had this experience, I would have always been searching for the love that could fulfill me. Possibly life might have presented me with a situation that would have taught me this lesson a different way, but I think that this individual and my relationship with this individual gave me the lessons I needed. And the next person who comes along will be another lesson. It will be very different. I already feel that my needs in life are different. I am very fortunate to be in a position where I can celebrate loving myself. How enriching that is to just celebrate me. I think I'm a much better person when I operate and engage with life and with people from this position.

Life has given me so many gifts. The more I recognize it, the more I feel the gratitude, the more abundance I notice. I think being in my forties is so brilliant, or maybe just accepting a difficult life lesson brings on this appreciation.

———————

I HAVE LEARNED so much from Yasmine. Accepting what is and sitting with it is a powerful practice. It amazes me what opens up when I do that. What I have learned from Yasmine's work in applied theatre is the power of looking at situations through the eyes of others, imaging what their life experience has been and how it has influenced how they see the world. A great deal of understanding opens up when we are able to loosen our grip on our own reality and start to see the reality of others by really hearing their stories and their perspective.

Questions for Self-Reflection

1. When Yasmine worked with young immigrants and refugees, she noticed that there was an erasure of sorts in order to fit in. What part of your personal heritage might you have erased to fit in?

2. Yasmine believes her Egyptian side makes her unique. What is the unique part of you that you are not celebrating? What can you do to recognize and celebrate that part of you?

3. Yasmine has noticed North Americans tend to exoticize differences rather than truly integrating them. How could you

better allow space for other people to authentically express their uniqueness?

4. In her relationship, Yasmine had to reckon with who she really was and what distinguished her from other people. Who are you really, and what values distinguish you from other people?

5. Yasmine values Canada because it embraced her. What and who do you most value in life? Why?

6. Yasmine feels that part of the allure of faith and traditions are that they build community. Being in relationship with a Canadian meant different traditions and faith, and she lost some of her culture and heritage. How do you build community? How are you embracing all of yourself in creating that community?

Love as a Premise for Life

JOCELYN MERCER

Co-president, Executive Producer at CJ Mercon

> 66 *Discipline equals freedom. Having discipline as a core value and taking actions that feel really true to me have resulted in me having a lot more freedom in my life, a lot more peace of mind.* 99

I KNEW VERY LITTLE about Jocelyn Mercer before we connected, yet I trusted Sheena's judgment completely. I smiled when Jocelyn described herself as a love bug, was awestruck by the trust and confidence she had in herself, and was overwhelmed by her willingness to share her story.

Jocelyn is a top-notch producer, a creative mind who exudes energy. Her creativity was nurtured from a young age by attending the Claude Watson School for the Arts, a specialized arts school that works to stimulate creativity and original thinking. Jocelyn develops and produces factual television, and is one half of CJ Mercon, which creates and builds character-driven digital brands on platforms like YouTube and Facebook that capture new audiences, connect with target markets, and maximize revenue. CJ's premiere brand is *How to Cake It* with Yolanda Gampp, a YouTube channel and lifestyle brand that in less than a year from its launch accumulated 1 million subscribers and 100 million views. The brand continues to grow at an accelerated rate of 150,000 new subscribers a month and is expanding rapidly into e-commerce and livestream events.

Jocelyn is a driver and creator of "big, juicy, tummy-tickling stories" with larger-than-life characters for all forms of visual media. She knows what she wants and she is learning to follow her intuition and inner guidance to get it. Her premise is love, and she does her best to align her business and life decisions with love. She assumes her premise for life to be true no matter what is going on around her and within her. Jocelyn let go of her belief that she was supposed to hold back her emotions, never taking the time to really feel. She gathered trusted friends around her so she could fully grieve her losses. She is open and keen to share her philosophies on life.

Key messages from Jocelyn:

- We all misstep. Be compassionate with yourself.
- Love your imperfections.

- Everything around us is our creation.
- Surround yourself with people who give you a fresh, positive perspective and see the possibility in you.
- Start moving in the direction you want and like-minded people will appear.
- Be open to receiving what you want in your life. For Jocelyn, that was love.
- Find good mentors.
- Take full responsibility for your life.
- Remember: Discipline equals freedom. Be consistent in your actions toward self-love.

———————

I AM A love bug. I am a lover. I am very loving. I just love, love, love. I love affection and I love people. I have a lot of love in my life and a lot of laughter and this is really important to me. I love space and I love decor and I obviously love storytelling and that is my work, my business. The premise of my life is love—100 percent. When I really understood how important love was to me, I automatically looked at how my life aligned with love. Anything in my life that didn't line up with love had to go—behaviour, projects, whatever. This made it so much easier for me to go, "Oh ya, this film doesn't line up and so I don't need to do that." If it doesn't line up with my premise, then I don't do it. Understanding that love is the premise of my life helped to ground me.

We all misstep. It's not like I'm always loving and everything is perfect. I can be a bitch. I can get mad. But because my premise is love, I've got to love that too. I've got to let myself do that and I've got to take a minute and go, "Okay, that didn't feel good, I didn't really like that. That didn't feel in line but it came out. Now, how do I want to act?" So it is not about being perfect, it is about understanding what my premise is so when I stray, I'm like, "Oh yeah, there's the mark and I'm going to find my way back." My premise pulls me back, it's like a magnet.

I was a single child of a single dad. My early life was pretty unstable. My mom suffered from addiction and mental illness. As unfortunate as it sounds, it had me daydreaming and visualizing all of these awesome things as a way to escape. It was a way to escape from how I was growing up. I am very fortunate, very loved. My family may not have been traditional. I didn't have the parental roles in my life like some people, but I was always loved and that was really awesome, for sure.

I grew up in the West Indies for part of my childhood. I went from Toronto to this little tiny island surrounded by water, and this created a sense of isolation that fuelled my need to imagine and create these worlds. It really served me and my job. I make TV. I make content for TV, for YouTube, for any platform really. I am a writer. I very naturally connect to the idea of visualization—really seeing it, feeling it, and almost tasting and smelling it.

I believe that everything around me is my creation. Everything around us is affected by our perception of it, by how we see it. It is our choice. When I need to "clear my slate," I close my eyes and go into what I call my white room. I imagine everything around me disappearing. There is just me and I am surrounded by white. It feels so liberating. My white room is a clean slate, a new beginning. Nothing in my world exists. It is just a blank canvas and I build from there. I visualize whatever I want to visualize.

What I notice now is as soon as that slate is clear, things and people pop into my mind. Sometimes I close my eyes and get in my white room and unexpected things happen. I believe our subconscious is quite powerful. I think when I create the white room in my mind, it creates a space for my subconscious to be heard more clearly. It allows me to create things that my subconscious needs to create for reasons I don't understand.

Dreaming is really intentional. I set aside time each day to dream. I dream when I walk. I dream when I drive. I make it a priority to think about something wonderful and to think about what I want, how I am going to get there, and how awesome it is going to be. You know, instead of the question "Who am I?" it's "Who can I be?" It is so much more limitless when you look at it this way. I like looking at it this way.

What I dream about is a feeling. After accomplishing some of the things I have visualized, down to the specifics, at the end of the day, when I get that thing I've dreamed about, nothing really changes. There is always something else that I want. What I have learned is that it's really a feeling I'm after.

I also write my gratitude list. I say thank you for the things I want that are not yet in my life. When I say thank you, it stirs up feelings and I get excited and become grateful and I get butterflies. This is really what we are after. I dream about feelings—feelings of inspiration, happiness, and fulfillment. I dream about being excited, being peaceful, and having peace of mind.

The people you surround yourself with are important. You really are the sum of the people who surround you. Take a look at those people. Surround yourself with people who provide you with a positive perspective. If you look at your life and realize maybe the people in your life aren't truly supporting where you want to go, let them be who they are. It's not about "they suck, get them out of my life." Love them for whoever they are and then find the people who really support where it is that you want to go.

If you start moving in a certain direction, like-minded people really become attracted to you. You have to be open to it. Sometimes as a dreamer, we can feel isolated, a little different and separate from others. I realized that there is no way I am the only person like this. I needed to open myself up and I needed to not let those thoughts of isolation and separateness upset me. I needed to be open to meeting other people who are like me. Visualize yourself connecting with like-minded people who are going to support your dreams.

Mentorship is so important. Find great mentors. Find those people and talk with them. Open yourself up to people who think the way you want to think. I have always had an angel. I have always had someone who has opened doors for me. I took responsibility for stepping through those doors and, you know, there were two more doors right after that one, and then three more.

Until I saw the movie *The Secret*, I had never thought of taking full responsibility for my life. I was thinking things like *My mom is an addict* and *I had to grow up so fast* and that kind of stuff. I used to feel like a victim. So that was a big turning point: really deciding that I was ready to let go. I became ready to take full responsibility for my life. By taking full responsibility for my life, it changed drastically. We have all had our struggles and you can't use those as a crutch for your entire life. The first thing was to get over the victim mentality. The second part was forgiveness. Forgiveness is a lifelong practice and I am still working on it.

I got out of a really crappy long-term relationship, a heartbreaking one, because it was with someone I really loved so it was hard to accept that it just hadn't worked. It was a relationship where I was really supported, both financially and emotionally. My whole life was that relationship, so when it ended I had to face the task of rebuilding my life. Then my mom passed away. I took the idea of responsibility a step further. I let myself open up and let myself be heartbroken and devastated. That's not something I had ever done before. I had always been strong and responsible—you know, impenetrable. I had always tried to be an adult. I really let myself feel that suffering and pain. That really changed my life. It really opened me up.

I moved in with my best friend until I could figure out my life. I asked for help. It is important to know when to ask for help. I said to my closest friends: "Look, I'm going to need you, and I'm probably going to annoy the hell out of you with how much I need you. Crying and doing God knows what, but I'll need you. I can't do this on my own and I need you to know this." That was important for me to do. They all got it. They all said, "Let's do this. I'm not worried. You're going to be great." You've got to surround yourself with people who believe in you, not with people who look at you with a sad face and feel sorry for you. You want to surround your-self with people who see the truth in you, the light, the possibility, and are willing to go through the ride.

I let myself sob on the bathroom floor for hours—to actually feel those things that I had never felt, that I had not let myself feel. When you really let yourself feel some of the feelings you have been avoiding all your life, it's not easy. It's really painful and traumatizing and yet I recognize that there is magic in it too. Now I look back on those moments as some of the very best in my life. You know, it's a choice. You can suffer all your life, and I watched my mom do that, or you can let yourself feel and let go. There is magic in this. I saw how it can transform you. It changed my life. I really opened up. That's when I stopped feeling isolated, separate, and different from everyone. I opened myself up to other people and new friends and my life expanded.

I really looked at my life and I thought, *Hold on a second—love has so much to do with it.* The reason why I really do anything, if I strip away the other words, is to be loved or to love. I believe that love is what drives humanity. Some might say that it is fear that drives us forward. Under fear is a fear of not being loved. We all want to be loved. Once I figured that out, I was like, *I need to make love a huge fucking priority in my life. I want to stand in love as much as I can. I want to love others as much as I can.* Love became my driving force. I have to remember that I don't need to look for love but I *do* need to be open to it. It is not something you have to go out and find. It is always there. All you have to do is be open to it. If you are open to love, it will be there.

I have a tattoo on my arm. It reads, *discipline equals freedom*. It is all about consistency. These are pure and simple concepts— whether it's standing in love or surrendering, or meditation, or whatever, those are core concepts you can work with in your life, day after day, year after year. Having discipline as a core value and taking actions that feel really true to me have resulted in me having a lot more freedom in my life, a lot more peace of mind. Consistency is a simple concept that the masters of our civilization understood. Action without consistency, one could argue, is useless. You must be consistent in your actions.

———

JOCELYN TAUGHT ME the importance of taking time to feel, to grieve. I had not thought much about my decision to leave my career as a loss or as something to grieve. I just kept doing, pushing myself forward. Yet there was so much to feel through before I could truly move on. When I took the time to deeply feel and reflect, I was able to come out the other side and be.

Questions for Self-Reflection

1. The premise of Jocelyn's life is love. What is the premise of your life? What would you like the premise of your life to be?

2. When Jocelyn dreams, it is about a feeling. She has learned that it's really a feeling she is after. How do you want to feel as you live your life?

3. Jocelyn surrounds herself with people who provide her with a positive perspective and support her where she wants to go. Who are the people who provide you with a positive perspective? Who

are the people in your life who see the truth, the light, the possibility in you, and are willing to go along for the ride—the good and the bad?

4. Jocelyn understood after getting out of a long-term relationship and the death of her mother that it was time to open up, and she let herself feel heartbroken and devastated. What are the emotions that you have not given yourself the opportunity to feel? How can you support yourself to feel them?

5. Instead of "Who am I?" Jocelyn suggests asking, "Who can I be?" That question opens up so many possibilities. So, who can you be? Be your limitless self as you consider this question.

Breaking Open Boxes

GLORIA ROHEIM MCRAE

Co-Founder of Wedge15 Inc., Brand Strategist,
Speaker, and Best-Selling Author

66 *Embrace the weird.* 99

GLORIA ROHEIM MCRAE and I met in Toronto for a coffee. She spoke of her ideal world being an open box. This really connected to what I was feeling, like I was stuck in a closed box looking for an airhole to catch my breath. She spoke with such clarity about herself, the diversity of her life, her worldview and perspective.

Gloria is an author, strategist, and speaker who is known for her bold approach. She began her career in public affairs after earning a bachelor of arts degree at McGill University and a master's degree in international affairs from the University of Toronto. She slowly transitioned into the not-for-profit and then private sector before starting her first company in 2010. Gloria is now the co-founder and chief strategic officer of Wedge15 Inc., which helps businesses, organizations, and teams leverage their brands for more impact and greater sales. She has fused her market research, public affairs, project management, and policy experience to become a powerful strategist at Wedge15, sought after for her interdisciplinary approach to project work.

Gloria speaks four languages fluently, is a regular *Huffington Post* columnist, and is a HuffPost Live commentator. She also appears in *Chatelaine* and *Glow* magazines and on Rogers TV and CTV. Her first book, BYOB: *The Unapologetic Guide to Being Your Own Boss*, became an Amazon.ca best-seller in entrepreneurship and self-esteem in October 2013, less than one month after publication.

She is a fast-talking, purpose-driven woman who sees supposed-to as a box imposed upon her—and she likes to break through those boxes. She celebrates differences and recognizes what makes us unique is our strength. Her parents' divorce, being raised in two different countries, and changing schools all the time are factors that she could have seen as liabilities. Instead, she focused on the strengths they brought her—the ability to see things differently, to celebrate change, and to learn several languages. She has made these assets her differentiator. By accepting all the pieces of herself, Gloria is able to create her own success.

Key messages from Gloria:

- We are here to experience joy and delight.
- Your difference, what is unique about you, is a strength, an asset, a differentiator. Embrace it.
- Try different things. It is the only way to find your passion.
- Approach life as a constant re-creation.
- Be yourself: unravel what has piled on the child who once dreamed.
- Tap into the magic of dreaming.
- Let curiosity fuel your dreams.

———

I'M ABSOLUTELY OUTSIDE of the box. I turned everything that makes me different into a strength, an asset, my differentiator. I built my life and my career around it. It is not about being different for the sake of it. Rather, it is about celebrating the differences that make me who I am. Some of these things include: the diversity in my family, the unique way my parents' divorce meant I was raised in both Hungary and Toronto, changing schools all the time, and speaking many different languages. These circumstances make up who I am. My childhood predestined me to see things from a different angle as an adult.

Boxes are constraining. It does not feel right when I am boxed or constrained by the limitations imposed upon me. I can endure boxes. I can put up with them, but it is not my preferred place of being. This is one of the main reasons I have left every job I have ever had. I tried being a policy adviser for one year, a market researcher for one year, a financial adviser for one year. I tried going abroad and doing international development work for about nine months, followed by a brief consulting gig, and then coordinated a not-for-profit project. All of these positions were really great and rich in possibilities. I gave each of them everything I had to offer at the time. But when I was first starting out, I explored. Everything about my life is about constant re-creation—of creating anew. I have to live life and try things because that is how I am going to figure out what I have to offer, not in a cubicle wondering while gazing out the window.

I'm always breaking open boxes whenever I have the opportunity. Sometimes this works to my benefit, and sometimes to my detriment. It doesn't matter, though, because I have space to be myself. I want to have space where there is love, compassion, and grace to be different for all of us and for myself. I am dreaming of a world of diversity and self-expression where the self-expression and differences are celebrated, a world where people are curious and open to these differences rather than afraid and averse to them.

My ideal world is an open box, a celebration, a gracious space for all kinds of different people to show up. It is a world where there is a curiosity to know people rather than to judge them against some personal standard. People are beautiful. If we all had the space, and were encouraged to dream, I would be excited to live in whatever that world would look like. Diversity, celebration, freedom, space, creativity, and self-expression are key to me. They inspire me. There is nothing more exciting than people living in what excites them. I may not know what they are talking about, but when they are lit up and alive, it's magnetic and life-giving to all of us.

I believe we are born to dream. We perceive the world at a young age from a very pure sense of self with a sort of innocence, without all the other crap that gets in our way later in life. I remember curiosity fuelling my dreams. I recall being very imaginative. I would imagine pictures of scenarios and desires in my life. When I became older, this became more complex and tangible. I would write or sketch something and share it with somebody instead of having it be this internal unspeakable vision.

I remember as a kid feeling limited by my cultural context of dreaming. You know when you are young everyone says, "That's not realistic, don't pursue that." There are so many distractions in our life—about how we are supposed to be, how we are supposed to act, what we should do, what we shouldn't do—that we forget how to dream. We believe at some point that dreams are not realistic.

I did stop dreaming at a certain time. I stopped dreaming when I became a jaded adult. I still had visions for things I wanted, but I just couldn't tap into the magic of dreaming. When I finished university, I bought a condo with my then boyfriend—my high school sweetheart—believing that was the way to fulfillment and happiness. I bought into that North American dream: get your education, a job, a good partner, buy a home. I became a property owner and a good employee. This was supposed to be the road to the good life. I hit a period of depression. I couldn't get out of bed on the weekends. I just questioned the point to my entire life.

I had pushed so hard to get there. Here's the loyal boyfriend, the good job, a salary, a mortgage, two degrees—isn't this the good life? Isn't this what I'm supposed to be celebrating? I had to start to deal with the fact that I was missing something key. I felt I had lost a connection to my dreams and my bigger purpose. It was a downward slope of anxiety for me then. Things shifted when I made a conscious choice at the age of twenty-five to change my lifestyle and adopt more personal development work. I broke up with my boyfriend and quit my job. I rediscovered my ability to dream. I spent time unravelling the things that had piled on top of the child within me who once dreamt.

Dreaming is essential to human well-being and fulfillment. You know, essential to passion, desire in life—the things we are here for. That's how I see a dream. It is kind of otherworldly. I get a vision of dreaming as if I am downloading from the universe. Everything that we have ever thought of or want already exists. It's about finding the magnet to pull it toward us. Can we pull ourselves toward it? Can we even believe it when we can't see how it's possible? We download into our human selves and then we seek opportunities in our life to express those dreams and experience them.

I think the people who are doing this are delighted. There is a delight to life, a joy to it. It's not that you don't have worries, or you don't have fears, because you are human. We learn to be fearful, to be scared, and yet we are here to experience joy and delight. We all have a different way of experiencing this, and this is what our journey looks like.

To me, dreaming is about creating a space to explore. The more I dream, the better I become at dreaming. Meditation helps me to get to a place of dreaming. I find that dreaming happens when you let go and release, when you allow wonderment to pass through you without judgment—whatever gets me to wonderment. I love how in community brainstorming, every idea is welcome. I love open spaces of exploration where people with distinct life experiences, people who have been exposed to different things, talk openly. One of the first lines in my book is, "We often call things weird or crazy when we can't understand them. I want to embrace the weird." To me, that would be a dream come true. When we all have space to fully express ourselves, we can all just kind of exhale. We can ditch the need to prove something and feel free.

I have deep desires where I will feel my heart or my insides call for me. I will take that calling and visualize it and then I will communicate it because at the end of the day, I need to make my dream happen. My dreams are not small. I need to be able to communicate these dreams, parlay them to other people so they can get excited about them too. I use my dreams as an anchor, a guide, a focus, and then I take action.

I met my husband and business partner and we started a company together in 2013. We make an incredible impact that fulfills me ten times more than a title and a cubicle. I have a life partner who is sensational. Now we have a son together too. Keon is another dream come true. We live the dream life in so many ways, though not according to the "North American prescription" for what a dream life is. We don't have the big house in the suburbs with the white picket fence, the dog, and whatever else. We live a very rich but very modest life. It is about making an impact for the next generation. It is different than if I had just followed the road that "they" told me to and got a "nice" job.

We don't get to where we are alone. Clearly, I steered the ship. My perceptions steered the ship, that is. Others nudged me and pushed me to the next step. My dad advocated for me. There were professors and other people who took a chance on me. Today when my doubts and fears overwhelm my bigger vision, my husband reminds me what I am forgetting in those moments. You know, when I am reticent to do something, he is the one who says, "That's yours, go get it." If everyone supports you and everyone agrees with what you are doing, you may be living their dream rather than your own. That could be okay, but realize that you are more wondrous and intuitive than you may think.

———

THAT BOXED-IN FEELING that Gloria described is exactly how I was feeling in my life. Gloria's metaphor of breaking through limitation really resonated with me. I discovered that the limitations I felt were ultimately self-imposed. I was the one choosing to stay in the box.

Questions for Self-Reflection

1. To Gloria, boxes are constraining. It doesn't feel right to her when she is boxed in by the limitations imposed on her. She lives absolutely outside the box. What boxes may be containing your life?

2. Celebrating differences makes Gloria who she is. It is her strength and her differentiator. Looking at your life experience, what makes you unique and different? What is your unique differentiator?

3. What are the unique differentiators, the strengths of the people around you? Try sharing with them what you see in them.

4. Gloria fills her space with love, compassion, and grace in order to experience full self-expression. Gloria does this by first feeling love, compassion, and grace. And she's not perfect—she knows she is a work-in-progress. What would you like your space filled with?

5. Gloria believes we are here to experience joy and delight. When have you experienced joy and delight? What were you up to? Who were you with? Where were you? What steps can you take to invite more of that joy and delight into your life?

Overcoming Expectations

DEVON FIDDLER

Founder and Chief Changemaker
at SheNative Goods Inc.

*66 Sometimes you have to let some things
go to achieve what you want to do. 99*

DEVON FIDDLER IS the youngest woman in the group,
yet her story is a powerful one. She is incredibly self-
aware. She described herself as "passionate, ambitious,
over-achieving, a bit of a dreamer, really optimistic, and then I
get disappointed when things don't happen the way I want it to
be. I'm sensitive. Sometimes I can be naive." I was struck by the
honesty in her description of herself and thought, *Oh yes, I have
experienced that disappointment when things don't happen the way
I want them to.*

Devon is Cree, a social entrepreneur from the Waterhen
Lake First Nation in Saskatchewan, and the chief changemaker
of SheNative Goods Inc. The SheNative brand of handbags and
accessories marries Devon's love of fashion with her desire to
give back to her community by changing the perceptions of Indigenous women and girls and empowering them at the same time.

Devon has a BA in Aboriginal public administration from the
University of Saskatchewan. She was recognized for business
and entrepreneurship by CBC Saskatchewan's 2015 Future 40
Under 40. Devon also represented Canada at the G20 Young
Entrepreneur Alliance (YEA) Summit in Istanbul.

Devon is rewriting the story of what it means to be an Indigenous woman by letting go of the low expectations society has of Indigenous youth. She recognized that she did not want to live out the cultural narrative that so many of her young friends had chosen when they dropped out of school. She powerfully chose her direction by changing schools and leaving her abusive relationships behind. She has not only empowered herself but now empowers others in her community. Devon was not afraid to experiment. She worked at different jobs and learned skills that helped her to discover and pursue her passion. She accepts failure as a tool for learning, growing, and improving—this perspective, along with her deep desire to help her community, speaks volumes for what this young woman will achieve.

Key messages from Devon:

- Grow beyond the expectations or limits placed on you.
- Sometimes a change in environment can make a huge difference.
- You know what is best for you. Follow your instincts.
- You may not find your "perfect" work right away. Keep experimenting.

- How you overcome your challenges may assist and empower others.
- Your life is a precious gift—don't spend it with someone who abuses you physically, mentally, or emotionally.
- People only change when they want to change. As much as we think we can change someone, the choice to change comes from the inside. We can't impose change on anyone. We can only change ourselves.
- Find the intersection between what you love and what your community needs.
- Ask for help. Find a mentor.
- There comes a moment when you say, "Yes, I'm going to do this."

———————

I DREAM OF a world where I am surrounded by all types of optimistic, fun, and excited people who are thinking about creating "the next big thing." I dream of people overcoming their circumstances and doing what they want to do. When I was a child, I dreamed of becoming a fashion designer but dismissed it when I went to university. I took political studies but didn't like it. My degree is in Aboriginal public administration. I studied this because I wanted to do stuff for my community.

As a child, I had a lot of non-Aboriginal friends. In middle school, there started to be cliques and groups. Most of the non-Aboriginal kids were grouped together and all of the Aboriginal kids were grouped. I started doing what was expected of me as an Aboriginal student—a lot of negative stuff. A lot of people don't have many expectations of Aboriginal students, so we end up doing what is expected of us. I ended up doing what I was "supposed" to do, like drinking and pretty much the typical teenager stuff.

I was a really good kid before that. I was a nerd. I got a 90 percent average in grade six. The next year my average dropped to 70 percent. That was my turning point, where I had become what was expected of me. I started becoming a bully to other girls because it made me feel more worthy or something. I made enemies. I am still trying to deal with that, trying to figure out how to make it right. Part of me broke out of my shell to become something different—a bit of a rebel. It was more like an alter ego or something. I don't know.

You still don't know who you are when you are young. My parents split during those years, one of my best friends moved away, and a lot of things like that happened within those middle school years. I just did what was expected of me and started being the bad kid. In high school, grade ten, there was a point where all of my friends were dropping out of school and most of them were First Nations. I felt like I didn't have many friends left. I just felt kind of alone. There was me and a couple of other friends. I started dating at the time. I was at a point in my life where I was skipping a lot of school and smoking weed. It was the only drug I was involved in. I was just generally getting into a lot of trouble. I nearly got kicked out of school in grade eleven for missing so many classes.

I begged my mother to let me go to school at our First Nation. It was about forty-five minutes from where we lived and my mother worked in the community. She let me go and I became more confident. I felt more accepted for who I was. I got better grades. Although the educational system comparably is at a lower standard, I thrived. I joined all the school organizations. I was on a couple of committees and I ended up being valedictorian.

I had a boyfriend in high school who was not a good influence on me. He got really mentally abusive and controlling. We lived together after high school while I did my first year of university. We ended up breaking up and I got into another unhealthy relationship with a younger guy. I think I wanted to be young, still feel like I was in high school. He was involved with gangs growing up. He told me stories about how he had treated his previous girlfriends. I wanted to be that person who would change him. It ended up not being that way at all. He eventually did get abusive. Partway through university, after this on-again off-again relationship, we called it quits and I started to thrive again.

I focused more on school. I got better marks. I decided what my major was going to be. I started making friends. I got involved in a lot of different things—the Indigenous Students' Council, and then I moved up to be the vice-president of Aboriginal relations in my final year. When I look back, I really notice how easily I could have gone downhill and stayed there. I changed things around, though.

After university, I fell into a job with the Tribal Council in a neighbouring community. It was there that I learned a lot about entrepreneurship. During that time I watched a friend of mine, Kendal Netmaker, start up Neechie Gear, a clothing brand that empowers Indigenous youth. That started opening my eyes to what you could do with entrepreneurship. I saw what he did and was inspired. I started thinking about what I wanted to do as a child and it all snowballed from there.

I decided I wanted to have a clothing line—Aboriginal women's business clothes. I entered a business plan competition and failed. Kendal, who had won an entrepreneur award years before, was up for an award at the same competition. Being there with him when he won the award was also inspiring. We took pictures together. It was really cool. I thought, *I want to be able to do this.* So that was the moment that made me say, "Yes, I'm going to do this."

I got into community development work and developed an economic development action plan for my First Nation. It was there that I started to come out of my shell. I started to facilitate workshops that helped me build my confidence. I also got the opportunity to go to the Indigenous Women and Community Leadership program in Antigonish, Nova Scotia. I learned that the reason I did terribly in my first business plan competition was because I knew nothing about the industry. I knew a little about business development and very basic entrepreneurship, but that was it. That program opened my eyes to the amount of work that goes into creating a business.

I asked Kendal if he would be my mentor and he said yes. I am finding out that even though he has created a path, my path is going to be completely different. I can't just do the same thing as he did because our businesses are not the same. Even though I am going to be a socially responsible company, he's doing sports and I'm doing a collection of handbags and I have a mission to empower Indigenous women so there are differences . . . a lot of differences.

I feel like you need to deal with all the skeletons in your closet, like any childhood traumas. It is a hard thing to do, but it will help in the future. Deal with your problems through counselling or whatever, so you are able to move forward, be a better you, and do what you want to do.

I'm learning to tell my story now because it is important. My business has a lot to do with me and my story. With SheNative, I'm seeking to empower Indigenous women and girls. SheNative marries my love of fashion with my desire to help my community. SheNative has so much to do with my circumstances. I believe that anyone can overcome their own circumstances if they believe in who they are and if they have the belief that they can do whatever they want. I think the world would be better off if people were able to rise above their circumstances and be all that they want to be. You cannot force people to do it. It has to come from within.

———

FROM DEVON I learned how clearly our life experience informs our purpose. All that we have lived, all the struggles we have encountered, prepare us for who we are becoming. We can wallow in the downward vortex blaming our circumstances for limiting us or we can choose the path of courage and create and re-create ourselves. We can look back and see our purpose clearly written in our past circumstances.

Questions for Self-Reflection

1. Devon lived with society's lack of expectations of Indigenous women and consciously decided they would not limit her. How are people's expectations or lack of expectations limiting you?

2. Devon had dismissed her love of fashion when she went to university. What passion may you have dismissed? How can you welcome it back into your life?

3. Reflect on the path you have walked in this life. Look for the moments in life that have informed you, inspired you, made you pivot in a different direction, those poignant moments or experiences that affected you in some way. All these moments are turning points. What are the turning points of your life? Write them down as you think of them. As we enter the upward spiral, we can start to see the messages in our past experiences that point to our purpose. What clues about your purpose are written in your turning points?

4. Devon knew that she would be better off at the high school in her community, and taking action to change schools was a turning point. It's important to develop skills of knowing what is best for us and acting on it. What is best for you right now? What are your instincts telling you?

5. At one point Devon said to herself, "Yes, I'm going to do this!" She committed to her dream. To what are you willing to say, "Yes, I'm going to do this!"?

Dream Beyond the Barriers

LISA BELANGER

Exercise Physiologist and Founder of
Knight's Cabin Cancer Retreats

> *Failure is not a bad thing.*
> *We are so afraid of failure, but failure is*
> *what we need to succeed.*

LISA BELANGER HAD a view of the Rocky Mountains while we spoke. The view from my window was not so spectacular. As I listened over the phone line, I imagined those mountains. Lisa learned at a young age to move beyond others' expectations and make decisions that align with what is most important to her. Her enthusiasm about this book reaffirmed my commitment to making it happen.

Lisa's passion for life is contagious. Driven by her interest in everything health-related, her goal is to show individuals, corporate groups, and other audiences how seemingly small lifestyle changes can have a profound impact on one's well-being. She has a PhD in behavioural medicine and is a certified exercise physiologist, a published author, a successful entrepreneur, and an entertaining keynote speaker. She is one of Edmonton's Top 20 under 30 and was awarded the YMCA Woman of Influence Local Hero Award.

Inspired by a teenage friend who passed away from cancer, Lisa founded the Canadian charity Knight's Cabin. Offered across Canada, Knight's Cabin is a cancer survivor retreat that focuses on physical activity, nutrition, sleep, and stress management. The program uses research-based information coupled with behavioural change science to produce lifelong health habits among retreat participants.

She has run a marathon in Paris, climbed Kilimanjaro with her father, and snorkelled the Great Barrier Reef—just a few of the activities on her ever-growing bucket list.

Lisa is very clearly in the driver's seat of her life, navigating her way and moving her life forward with passion and stubborn optimism. She has chosen to follow her passion rather than be limited by the expectations of others. She turns stumbles, setbacks, or mistakes that arise along the way into opportunities to regroup, refocus, and try a new method. She took a right turn off the academic track, giving up what she felt an academic was supposed to do with a PhD—become a professor— and instead pursued what truly brings her joy—working with cancer survivors.

Key messages from Lisa:

- Imagine what it would be like to create the life you want.
- Create a bucket list of all the places and things you want to experience.
- Take steps to *experience* your bucket list, not just check off items. Experiencing your bucket list is the difference between jumping off a bus, taking a photo of the Coliseum, then jumping back on the bus versus getting off the bus, leisurely walking through the Coliseum, imagining what it must have been like to see gladiators fighting, then finishing with a picnic outside the Coliseum with people you met.
- Be aware of the barriers you have constructed for yourself.
- Take down those barriers and limits, and dream big.
- Transform your biggest hurt in life into your motivation to make change in the world.

———

I WAS EIGHTEEN years old when my best friend, Jane, was diagnosed with cancer. When she was sick, she couldn't do much. Travel became her big dream; she wanted to travel everywhere. She hadn't talked about travel much before she got sick, but being in bed, not being able to venture more than a 20-kilometre radius from her house, really fed her desire to travel. Jane went from being accepted into nursing school to deferring for one year, and began working as a waitress so she could raise money to travel for six months.

When Jane was sad or having a bad day, we looked at pictures of far-off places and imagined what it would be like to be there. As an analytical person, I really hadn't done much imagining before. Dreaming is not something that comes naturally for me, but talking about travelling was something I could do to make Jane feel better.

We would go for walks and imagine what it would be like to share a glass of wine in Paris. We didn't even know if we would like wine, but it seemed like a good idea to sip wine together in Paris. We imagined what it might be like to live in Paris for a year. We started to look at life so differently. I think that is what you do when you are faced with death. You go, *Holy crap, what is life? Is it this 9-to-5 right now? Is it going to university right after high school? Will it be the end of the world if I go travelling?* Jane questioning things like that really taught me to show up differently in the world.

Jane and I made a bucket list of things we wanted to accomplish together. I now have my own bucket list, and it has made the impossible in my world not impossible anymore. I am determined to experience everything that is on that list and I am so, so grateful for it. I made it public. I did this so people will know when I check them off. And it is not just about checking them off. I feel everything on the list has a story and that is what makes this list so powerful. It is not just about checking the thing off. It is about the adventure along the way. It is the people you meet. The stories they tell. It is cool. It is powerful. It has helped me to be comfortable with the uncomfortable.

I grew up in the Maritimes and dreaming was very much encouraged by my culture, and yet at the same time people are taken aback if you take steps to accomplish your dream or step beyond the norm. We were told that "you could do anything you want," as in only these eight professions available to you, and that "you know you can dream big," but not too big. So I found it ironic that people would say, "If you could be or do whatever you want, what would you do?" If you came up with these ideas like, "I want to change the health-care system," then people say, "Whoa, whoa—too big. You dream too big and that's outside my comprehension. I don't like it." So as a whole—and obviously there are people who support dreaming big and get behind it—but as a whole, I don't know if it is encouraged.

Growing up in my community meant having 2.5 kids, the picket fence, the middle to upper middle income. Everybody had a profession. You could pinpoint exactly what they did. It wasn't entrepreneur. It wasn't start-up. It was lawyer, doctor, producer, accountant. They were all very defined roles. The mindset, which was truly modelled by our parents, is to go away to school for four, eight, or whatever number of years. You get your designation and you return to the community, buy a house, and start a family. That's how it goes. We were never encouraged to investigate beyond this defined formula.

I was able to dream beyond the barriers that I constructed for myself when I was growing up. Only you can put limitations on yourself and on your abilities. Your limitations are like a fence around you. If that fence is only eight feet away, that's where you will go. What it took for me to move beyond that fence, beyond those limitations, was seeing my friend die. That experience created within me an emphasis on life. Experiencing the adventures from the bucket list Jane and I had created together is a constant reminder to continue to take down the barriers I have created for myself. I encourage everyone to look at the barriers they have constructed for themselves and just take them down. Others have done it, so why can't you?

I think that dreaming is encouraged; it's just that people are almost afraid of dreams because what if it doesn't work? What if you fail? Like failure is a bad thing. I truly believe that it is not. The culture of academics, you can't get published if you don't have positive results. Aren't negative results just as important so somebody doesn't go and try to do it again? We are literally failing all over the world in the exact same way because nobody is taking the step to or able to publish the failure. Now there are journals that are coming out on just that—on failures so we can learn from them. Failure is what we need to succeed and that is not taught in our school system. People are not learning how to fail properly, so failure is something that can be extremely positive, extremely beneficial if you know how to fail. If you just try to hide it under the bed and then move forward without really, truly learning that lesson or experiencing that failure, it's pointless. It is: "Unfortunately you failed. Pick yourself up again and take the lessons learned."

I have been an academic for many years and I would say that it creates similarly limiting beliefs. "Be innovative—whoa, whoa, too innovative. I don't like that." When you apply for grants, you are told to add a tiny bit about research that has already been done. Don't think differently. Don't come from a different angle.

One very positive thing about academics is you learn how to take criticism. That's what you do daily. When you are working on research, another academic comes in, reviews your work, and rips it apart. Criticism becomes such a positive thing because it makes your work better. The power of criticism is not typically taught.

After ten years of school, I began interviewing for professorships at some really good schools. My husband asked, "Why are you miserable?" I realized that the better I become at "being a professor," the less I will talk to people. When you are a student, you do all the grunt work. For me, the grunt work was working with cancer survivors, which I love. My professor was the best in the world and all he does is write all day. He'll come out for meetings maybe. So I realized that I don't want to be there. If I excel at what I do, I will hate my job.

My husband then asked, "If you could do anything, *anything*, what would you do?" This is not a question that gets asked very often. Few people take the time to ask, "What does success mean to you? Take everything else out, erase everything that you have come to know about society, including what is acceptable. What would you do?" When I answered, I almost surprised myself. I said I would do this cancer retreat and I would fight for the idea of having it within the health-care system.

Then he asked, "Why don't you do that?" and I became a stuttering fool. I am very rarely at a loss for words, yet I couldn't give him a good enough answer for "Why not?" I realized that I had finally been asked what is my dream, and to not be able to provide a sound reason as to why I couldn't go out and do it right now, that was pretty huge for me. So I did it.

When I think of dreaming I always think big, like I hope this happens on a greater scale and I'm going to create it. I'm going to start things and yet it's not dependent on me. Other people can take it over and keep it going.

———

LISA HAD ME looking at my own life to discover the cultural and family beliefs that had been imprinted on me. I could see similar patterns in my upbringing. Our family success formulas were similar. I also know I received a message in life to dream big but not that big. It is easy to dream big; it is another thing to act into that big dream. I ask myself regularly now, *If you could do anything, what would you do?*

Questions for Self-Reflection

1. Seeing her friend die enabled Lisa to move beyond the fence—the limitations she had constructed for herself—and to dream beyond those limitations. How would you describe the fence you have placed around yourself? How high is it? What is it made of? How much space does it provide you to explore? What is one thing you could do today to start to take the fence down or move it a few more inches away from yourself so you have more space for exploring and experimenting in your life?

2. Lisa spoke about her family formula of having 2.5 kids, the picket fence, the middle to upper middle income, and a profession.

What was your family formula? How does it align with who you are today? How does it align with who you can be, who you are becoming?

3. Lisa has shifted her definition of success a few times. She let go of her family's definition of success with her choice to work toward a PhD in behavioural medicine. She then shifted her definition of success by letting go of the idea that she needed to continue in academics and become a professor. What does success mean to you today? How has your definition of success changed over time?

4. Academics taught Lisa the power of criticism to make her work better. What is your relationship to criticism? What criticism have you heard that has the power to make you or your work better?

5. "If you could do anything, *anything*, what would you do?" This is the question Lisa's husband asked her that got her in touch with what was really important to her and changed the direction of her life.

6. Lisa has made her bucket list public. What is on your bucket list? Who are you going to share it with?

Forgiveness Letters

NICKOLETTE REID

Visual Merchandizing Lead and Image
and Empowerment Advocate

> 66 *If I can see it in my head and feel it in my heart, it's already mine.* 99

NICKOLETTE REID IS an absolute treasure. While speaking with her, I had the urge to jump down the phone line and give her a big hug. Nickolette's story could so easily be one of disempowerment and hardship. Her ability to shift perspective and willingness to seek out the source of her challenges has made her story an empowering one. As we spoke on the phone, she was cuddling with her dog, Jake.

Nickolette is an image expert. Growing up in the fashion industry, she learned the power of image to create success. She is the author of *The Power of Image* and has developed programs and workshops to teach women and men how creating their best image in turn creates their best life. She has written style and fashion articles for various fashion magazines and has been featured on *Breakfast Television*, Slice Channel, and CTV. Nickolette's passion is helping people to create personal empowerment through visual success. She works with the Toronto District School Board to provide image, etiquette, and coaching workshops. Her favourite retreat is to cuddle with Jake after a long day at work.

Nickolette lives from a place of purpose and openly shares her story to help others. Her story is a courageous journey into self-awareness. She learned the hard way about the importance of taking time to nurture, rejuvenate, and heal. By shifting the way she viewed life, she was able to move forward in her own life. By shifting her perspective, Nickolette discovered the freedom that forgiveness brings.

Key messages from Nickolette:

- Live with purpose.
- Know you are enough.
- Live like you know that whoever created you did not make a mistake.
- Pause, retreat, reflect.
- Nurture yourself.
- Believe in something bigger than yourself.
- Disentangle yourself from your beliefs by shifting your perspective and finding forgiveness.
- Act boldly.

I LIKE PURPOSE. I must have purpose. I wake up and I have a purpose. I don't do things willy-nilly. That doesn't fly with me. I think my purpose has changed often, but at my core, my purpose is relatively the same. When I was working for my mother, she had a design and dressmaking firm. My purpose was not to work for my mother and not to do anything in the fashion industry. Everyone kept telling me that I was going to be just like my mom. I was like, "No, I am different."

When I graduated from school, I realized that it was natural for me to know about what looks good on others. It's innate. Around me I would see women juggling many things. When I would ask them how they are doing, they would often reply, "I'm tired." They always seemed very run-down. I would think, *If I add a little bit of this colour or that accessory to your outside, you would feel so much better and feel better about yourself.* I opened my image-consulting firm. My purpose at this time was to work with as many clients as possible to help make their wardrobes work better for their lives. I realized that by helping in this way, I wasn't scratching the itch. My purpose slowly evolved into helping people from the inside out. We can talk about the outside, that's fine. But if you really want to create a lasting impact on others, then you must begin from the inside. I decided to get to the root cause of why they were wearing those clothes. Then I evolved again.

I was watching a documentary about a young girl who had died from anorexia. When her mother and sister went into her room, there were posters of fashion magazines and models. It hit me because it really bothered me. I thought, *I am a part of this, this death cycle. I am feeding this negative monster in the minds of young girls and women.* This "I'm not good enough" monster believes she is not tall enough, or the "right" colour, or religion, or whatever. It is a constant—I'm not good enough. You know, seeing that girl's room was like seeing blood on the wall. I was like, "I can't only be for the haves. I want to reach as many people as possible."

Then my business began to morph again. I started believing that I needed to help more people, rather than only those who can afford my services. So I started conducting free workshops and I stopped working with clients one-on-one. I started attending conferences and networking functions. I wanted to effect change on a larger scale. I went on tour. I did a whole lot of speaking. I wrote a book. I spoke about no matter who you believe created you—God, Buddha, Ganesh, Allah, whoever it is—they did not make a mistake. Trees don't worry about being watered. Birds don't worry about where their food will come from. Why are we worrying? Stop worrying so much. I heard people say, "Nobody will love me because of how I look." What? It doesn't matter. I would tell them, "Are you serious? If they are not going to love you because of something like that, do you really want them in your life?" My view is if you don't love me when I'm down, you don't deserve me when I'm up.

I started speaking publicly and there was a huge marketing campaign associated with it. It was amazing, the best time. I was working constantly because it was such a mission. It was my passion. It was my Noah's Ark, my everything. Sadly, I became very ill. I was diagnosed with thyroid cancer. It was a good thing, though, trust me. I learned so much. I cannot tell you how much I learned. This was one of the best things to ever happen to me. I learned to slow down and embrace moments.

When I was diagnosed, I was like, "What did you say?" Then my type A personality was asking, "How does this happen? Fix it. Find the source." That's my thing. "Let's find the source of this problem." I did genealogy tests, looked six generations back. I got everybody in my family to get blood tests. I needed to figure out what was going on because cancer is not prevalent in my family—hypertension, high blood pressure, and heart attacks are, but not cancer. Then I started doing research about stress levels and discovered stress can cause disease. My life was happy, but I was stressed. I felt I had to do more. I was constantly thinking that I wasn't doing enough. After my operation, I put my business on hold. As an entrepreneur, you are your business. When you are not there, you are wondering, *What's going on? What's happening?* When you are a speaker, it is even more prevalent.

They removed my entire left thyroid. I couldn't speak for four months. It was hard. It was the worst four months ever. When I could speak again, I was like, "Okay let's get back to the grindstone." Four months later the sucker came back. I was diagnosed with cancer of the right thyroid and it was spreading to my throat. I indignantly asked it: "I don't smoke, I don't drink, so what are you saying to me?" This is not happening to me. I started to investigate: "Okay what's the message? What's the source?" Then I realized that I hadn't learned my first lesson. I hadn't slowed down. As soon as I got the okay, I was already booking appointments. Then I realized, "Okay, I've got to pump the brakes on this." I sold my business. I learned about food. I used to be 240 pounds.

The second round was really dramatic. It was very invasive. I went through chemo. I did radiation. I lost a lot of weight. It was scary. I was thinking, *I'm not going to argue anymore. I'm not going to fight anymore.* I made peace with the idea. I read a lot. I started doing meditation and slowing down my life. I started to pay attention. I realized that I was holding on to things—thoughts, feelings, and emotions. I wasn't being honest. Now, if I want to be quiet, I want to be quiet. If I want to laugh, I want to laugh. That year was just amazing. I think that once in a while you need to take time off and just cut the world off and back up and try this again. I did that and it was great. At that point in time, I definitely figured out who I am. I went to the Dominican Republic on vacation by myself. This was a big move for me. It turned into another shifting moment. I know that it helped to change things and I can see the ripple effects today. I went on that trip to "bury the dead," and let go of the past. I went to the Dominican with a new journal and I wrote "I forgive you" letters to a few key people in my life.

On my trip, I started noticing that anytime a person would talk about their parent, mother or father, it would reopen a wound, and I felt it in my stomach. I had to really think about why certain things had happened to me and I had to forgive the people involved in order to move on. I could not open to the good things that were possible for me because I was holding on to bitterness. Trust me, in the beginning that anger, that hatred, that disgust, fuelled me. It fuelled me to move further, it fuelled my independence. I am fiercely independent. It's like almost thirty years later—bury it already. So I wrote the "I forgive you" letters not for them but for me.

People did certain things to me because they didn't know better. My justification prior to the vacation was, "Well, they should have known better. You don't do that to people you are supposed to love." On the trip I realized these people did that to me because someone who was supposed to love them did that to them. So you can't be mad at them. That is where they are pulling from. They are pulling from the diseased pool of how to love. So you can't be mad at them. That diseased pool is their only source of how to love.

It is a cycle and you can't get mad at somebody who doesn't know any better. If they don't have the knowledge, then you can't be mad. I wrote, "I get why you did that to me. Your mother did that to you. Your father did that to you. I forgive you. It is not your fault. I get it. I get it, and from this day forward our relationship is on a clean slate."

The moment I did that, I can't tell you the relief I felt. I wrote their name on the letter. I tore each letter up and I let them go in the ocean. I sat there in the water sobbing. It felt so good. I let everything go into the ocean. I thought, *Well, the ocean is big enough to take this problem. It's not mine anymore.* That was a huge turning point in my life. No more anger at people. No more "I don't like you, I don't trust you, you hurt me." I'm done with that. I'm done with that.

FROM NICKOLETTE I learned the importance of pausing, asking, "What's the source?" and reflecting. What I have discovered is that the answer may be uncomfortable. When I have truly sat with it and reflected, the finger invariably gets pointed my way. To recover from my burnout took a long pause and a lot of self-reflection and required me to blow up some of my beliefs and behaviours.

Questions for Self-Reflection

1. It was natural for Nickolette to know what looked good on other people, and she has made a career that she loves from what is innate for her. What is innate for you? What do you just naturally do or notice?

2. When Nickolette saw the documentary of the young girl who died of anorexia, she felt compelled to reach out to as many as she could with the message, "You are perfect just the way you are." It was her Noah's Ark, her way of helping others. What's your Noah's Ark? What do you feel strongly compelled to do or to create?

3. Nickolette learned to slow down and embrace moments. How might you need to slow down? What moments could you be embracing?

4. Nickolette came to the realization that people behaved the way they did toward her because that is what they were taught by their parents and life experiences. They don't know any better. With that shift in perspective came the ability to forgive. What would you need to understand about people's situations in order to shift your perspective and find a sense of forgiveness?

5. Nickolette wrote "I forgive you" letters to people, not for them but for her. In writing the letters and letting them go in the ocean, she broke a cycle and opened to a new definition of love and relationships. What would your "I forgive you" letters say?

Writing Yourself into Being

CHRISTINE DERNEDERLANDEN

Author, Certified Trauma Services
Specialist, and Life Coach

66 Anything is possible if you dream it. If you dream it and you believe it, you can do it. 99

CHRISTINE DERNEDERLANDEN called me up at work one day. She shared the dream that she had always had of owning a toy store and at the same time wanted to help the environment. She wanted to know whether the company I worked for had any waste toys she could pick up. The company had a public waste depot and we were always looking for ways to reuse and recycle what was dropped off. Christine's call and her dream to sanitize, refurbish, and repackage toys for resale was a perfect fit for us. I knew that a lot of toys were thrown away, and more than likely we could separate them for her to have a look at. We did just that, and a long-term relationship was developed that diverted toys from the landfill and helped to birth the Toy Doctor, the toy company Christine had always dreamed of. When I decided to interview her, I thought that I would be hearing about how she had dreamed up the Toy Doctor. Her story was quite a surprise and far more powerful than refurbishing toys.

Christine is the award-winning author of *Where Is Robert?*, the grief kit that aided more than six thousand families affected by 9/11. She was honoured with a Certificate of Appreciation from former U.S. secretary of defense Donald Rumsfeld for her work in the aftermath of 9/11. Christine is also the author of *Where Is My Courage?*, a book that helps children cope with life's challenges and aided children in the wake of the Fort McMurray, Alberta, fires of 2016. She is also the creator of H.U.G.S., a program aimed at helping children understand grief. H.U.G.S. was inspired by the grief camps she facilitated with the Friendship Ambassadors who bring dialogue annually to the United Nations and Lions International.

Christine was profoundly affected by her brother's death and turned to writing to heal her pain and loss. She knew that the story of how she managed her grief could help others, and it has in a big way. With death as her constant companion, she left fear behind and learned to fully live. In doing so she provides an excellent example of a woman who has let go of supposed-to. She is in a constant cycle of creating and re-creating herself.

Christine is a certified trauma services specialist and has been recognized internationally for her work as a humanitarian in the field of grief and trauma. Her great passion is helping children, adults, and families cope with grief and trauma. She was awarded the 2001 Standard Literary Prize for her article

"Putting All My Problems in Perspective." Christine is also a licensed hairdresser, trained in cosmetology, fashion, and makeup artistry. She has appeared in various movies and as a television host. She has professionally modelled, is the owner of a truck parts supply corporation, and continues to inspire others as an empower coach. The success of Robert's Press noted her as one of Niagara's most successful businesswomen, a finalist for Woman of the Year and Entrepreneur of the Year in 2001.

Christine challenges everything. She is a firecracker who continues to evolve. She is a perceptive, intuitive adventurer who is not afraid to "try things on" and is not worried about what other people think.

Key messages from Christine:

- What we decide about an event in our past can affect how we live into the future.
- Writing can help with healing.
- The story of your healing journey can heal others.
- Don't believe the naysayers.
- Sometimes our biggest traumas provide our gift for the world.
- Leave fear behind.
- Try things out.
- Take a break to reflect and rebuild your soul.

I REMEMBER WHEN I was a teenager. I was in the backyard with my brother. He was sitting on a concrete slab and I was standing in front of him. We were talking about what we were going to do with our lives. "I'm going to grow up and be something that I don't have to work so hard at," I said. I always felt that my parents were working so hard at everything, trying to make ends meet, and they were successful at it. I wanted to do something that required a little less work. I aspired to model, to act. I dreamed of a world that was a lot different than I had. When my brother died, this dream fell to the ground. I was in grade eight when my brother went to Niagara Falls with friends. He hopped a fence to go pee and ended up falling into the Niagara Gorge. His body was found the next day by tour boat operators.

When my brother died, I felt like I had done something to deserve it, that I must have been bad, that it was my fault. After he died, I got sick with osteomyelitis, an inflammatory disease that affects the bone and bone marrow. I thought that my sickness was punishment. I felt like I was being continuously punished for his death. I had an ongoing fear that if I did love again, that the people I loved would die.

His death, and what I decided about it, was a hurdle that I have faced in every aspect of my life. I wanted to fill the void in the family. I wanted to be the child whom they missed. A minister once said to me, "Do you ever think that, perhaps, God and humanity were standing beside you when your brother fell in the Gorge? They were not pushing him?" That changed my perspective. I did not do something wrong to deserve this.

To deal with my brother's death, I started to write. I wrote and wrote. It was my way of overcoming. I declared, "I'm going to be a writer." People told me that there was no way I could be a writer and I told them, "Yes, I can." I wasn't very good in school. I struggled and was bullied. A lot of people told me no one would ever buy a book about death and dying. I wrote *Where Is Robert?* anyway and created my own publishing house and began marketing the book.

After my brother died, my dream was to help people realize that they are not alone in their traumas. When I established Robert's Press—helping people through life's challenges—my goal was to make sure that no one felt alone in my community. With Robert's Press, I started to share this dream with people and I began noticing that people jumped on board and started helping.

Large bookstores wouldn't even carry the book; they said it wasn't marketable. When the World Trade Center in New York City came down, everything changed. An emergency response worker from the United States ordered as many *Where Is Robert?* grief kits as possible. The grief kit includes the book *Where Is Robert?*, a plain white memory box, crayons, and a memory journal. The book encourages children to capture their special memories in writing, drawings, and objects that remind them of the person who died, just as Chrissy does in the book. I ended up deploying to New York City to assist the emergency response team with death notifications. I helped to develop healing camps for kids and families, and supports for teachers who were being asked difficult questions about death after the tragedy. The fact that *Where is Robert?* went international, and I ended up at 9/11, and that I was able to touch so many people is just fascinating to me. It was just unbelievable. I even received a certificate of appreciation from the Pentagon for my work after 9/11. It is mind-blowing that one person could do this.

When I came home from New York City, I had left fear behind. To my husband's surprise, I declared, "I'm going to ride a motor-cycle." I bought one and I learned how to ride it. Then I said, "I'm going to be a TV reporter." He said, "You can't just be a TV reporter." I called up Cogeco, the local cable channel, and said, "I would like to be a TV reporter." I became one, and I ended up getting paid for other acting gigs. I even starred in a movie and then after that I was like, "Wow, anything is possible." If you dream it and you believe it, you can do it. It's the believing part that you must start with. While everybody is telling you, "No, it can't be done," you just have to believe it. If you really believe it, it starts to come true.

The interesting part now is that when I talk about death, I am just so comfortable with it. I have been with people when they die. I have been with family members who are dying, and they take their last breath right in my arms. I could do this every day for the rest of my life. People ask me, "Aren't you sad?" I have learned to connect with myself, and perhaps with those people, either spiritually or perhaps through meditation, so I still let those people guide me, those people are still there. You just have to reach out and grasp that. It's just like birth. The moment a child is born is much like when a person dies. When children are dying, they talk about the things that they see—loved ones and everything around them. They become ultimately comfortable with dying. It's amazing how, when a child dies, they are just so okay and they can actually look at you and say, "Goodbye." I just say, "Okay, goodbye," and it is phenomenal. It makes me think of the afterworld a lot.

I am a bit sick of the death field. But as much as I want to leave it, it is part of me. I can't really walk away from it. I need to find a different element of it. For me, saving the planet means saving a human being. I did leave it at one point, and this is hilarious. I left my career because I felt that I couldn't do it anymore. So I came home and got a job as a manager of a lingerie store. I was like, "Okay, I am going to integrate back into society." That's what I thought. I took the job as manager and I got in trouble the first time because I had arranged a TV or radio interview. I got in trouble with upper management because I was not following the corporate guidelines. I arranged the interview because I was trying to market the store. Apparently, the guidelines did not allow media interviews.

My next idea was to conduct a sales competition where the winner would choose a product of a certain value. I got in trouble for that as well. My boss said to me, "You know how when a person experiences cancer, they can't go back to life as usual? You are like a person who has experienced cancer and you can't go back." I asked, "Go back to what?" and she replied, "Just being an employee." I think they wanted to fire me, so I quit. Under my management, I had increased sales over 50 percent, so I didn't understand why they would let me go. That's when I realized I was on the wrong track. When you go down the wrong path, everything is an obstacle, a fight. That job was so draining to me. Every time I tried to take initiative, something was in my way stopping me.

Right now I am taking a mini sabbatical. I wrote down the things I want to change in my life, including my finances, my emotional and spiritual connection with others, and my diet. In the past, when I was deployed as a certified trauma specialist, my bosses would tell me to take some time off and would send me to a retreat where I would heal. When I returned home, I would think to myself, *Well, I'm home now and I'm not going to do that anymore so I won't need those retreats.* I then realized I needed a retreat. What if I was able to take a moment and step out of my life, and still do what I do? What if I could step out of the routines of life and see where I am? So I did that. I feel so much better and now I am reaching out to others while deep into my career, back into the things I feel and care about. I am now standing on solid ground.

Upon reflection, I now have a different perspective. I realize that it is about me. It should have been about me the whole time. In order to care about others, we must first care for ourselves. I wanted to be what was expected of me. Now I know that if I care for me, and I love my body, I take care of it. I eat properly and I take time to rebuild my soul because sometimes my soul hurts.

———

IT IS A powerful thing to write yourself through a challenge and into your next becoming as Christine did. Writing is transformational. Without realizing it, I was writing myself through grief and loss as I wrote this book. As I wrote and rewrote, I moved through some challenging emotions into peace. I moved through confusion and into clarity. I shifted from a fearful, survival mind to an accepting, thriving mindset. I wrote myself into my next becoming.

Questions for Self-Reflection

1. After her brother died, Christine decided that it must have been her fault that he died and that she had to be the best daughter to her parents to make up for the loss of their son. She lived in continuous fear that the people she loved would die. When Christine heard the question, "Do you ever think that, perhaps, God and humanity were standing beside you when your brother fell?" her perspective changed and she reconsidered her beliefs about her brother's death. When may you have made a decision about an event in your life that may be holding you back today? What perspective shift about that event could change the decision you made about the event?

2. When I interviewed Christine, she was on sabbatical to rebuild her soul. What things do you do to rebuild your soul? How do you know when it's time to take a retreat?

3. Prior to going on sabbatical, Christine wrote down things she would like to change in her life and got support to address them. What are the things you would like to change in your life? How would you like them to change? Who could support you in creating those changes?

4. Christine has tried out a number of jobs—TV reporter, writer, model. Make a list of the things you have always wanted to do. Pick one of those things. What is something you could do right now to start to make it happen?

5. Christine uses meditation to connect with herself and with others for guidance. How do you connect to your inner guidance system? Where can you make time to do that more regularly?

Mindshift into Success

KAMINI JAIN

Olympian, World Cup Medallist, and Coach

> 66 *When we are aware that we control the imagery, and the imagery does not control us, then it becomes a tool for us rather than the enemy.* 99

I BABYSAT KAMINI JAIN when I was a teenager in Calgary, Alberta. I remember her and her sister climbing all over me when I walked through the door. We met again at Royal Roads University, where we both were studying for our master's degrees in leadership. Kamini interested me not only because she was an Olympic athlete but also because she could so clearly communicate her feelings without triggering others. I thought she, as a master paddler, would definitely have a perspective on using dreaming and visualization to create success.

Kamini was born in Tripoli, Libya, and moved to Canada at the age of four. She was a member of the Canadian National Kayak Team for nine years and has eleven World Cup medals and two Olympic finals. She also has two master's degrees, one in physiology and the other in leadership, and a dog named Taro who seems to spend as much time on the water as Kamini. Kamini sees sport as a way for people to expand their boundaries, live without limits, and gain empowerment by proving their physical strength and mental discipline. Her coaching objective is to encourage paddlers to set ambitious goals and provide them with the tools to perform their absolute best and fulfill their objectives.

Kamini has raced and coached sprint kayaking, outrigger canoeing, and dragon boating. Combining high-level training and full-time coaching in a variety of paddling disciplines has allowed Kamini to examine paddle sports in a way that few people have had the opportunity to do. Kamini has a video series on Vimeo called *101 Ways to Think About Paddling*, where she encourages paddlers to think creatively or playfully, as well as practically, when moving their craft.

Kamini is focused. Even her communication style is clear, concise, and direct. The precision and focus required by her sport is obvious in the way she presents herself. She exudes strength, balance, and groundedness and yet still knows how to have fun. Through sport, Kamini has gained a clear understanding of how our thoughts and beliefs can get in the way of our performance and cause roadblocks in our lives. Hanging on to what we believe we are supposed to do to excel can actually limit our success.

Key messages from Kamini:

- Be aware of your thoughts and imagery.
- Shift your self-talk to support you.
- Technique can be more important than speed.
- Create your thoughts and imagery, don't let them create you.
- Notice the roadblocks you have constructed for yourself.
- Be aware of the process outside yourself that may define the best way for you to achieve your goals.
- Make time and space for balance.
- Ask for help.

———

AS AN EXTREME introvert, I used sport as a way to be seen. With a team sport, you could sit on a bench because you maybe weren't as outgoing or as good. But a racing sport was like, "Here is your stage. Do with it what you can." That is what pulled me toward kayaking. I could be seen and I could develop an identity. In the sport of kayaking, your boat is really tippy. It is also very technical, and you have to be focused. It's almost an introvert's dream.

I grew up not feeling recognized. It was internal. I think it was also part of growing up an immigrant in a very white neighbourhood. I had a name that nobody ever bothered to learn to say properly. My parents were hardworking and, as I recall, not particularly physically affectionate. That is not a criticism. It is just the way they are. I was extremely shy, so I don't think I ever felt special.

At a young age I had this picture of an Olympian as somebody who was worthwhile. I got this idea, one, from the movie *Chariots of Fire* and seeing how impressed my mother was by the athletes in the story. I saw that movie at age eleven and was really inspired by it. The second thing I remember vividly happened when I was probably ten or so. I was in a tent outside with the twins who lived next door and they told me that their father had come an inch short of being on the high jump team for the 1964 Olympics. They also said he could jump over the house. I thought, *So that's how you impress these girls next door. You go to the Olympics.* The funny thing was that their dad was also an extremely successful surgeon. For some reason, the surgeon didn't stay in my head, but the fact that he could jump over the house and almost made the Olympics did.

I became a paddler because I watched the 1984 Olympics on TV and they showed the paddling because the Canadian team was doing really well. After watching it so many times, I decided, *I'm going to try that.* We lived right by the canoe club so it was easy to try.

I would describe myself as an immigrant growing up in a culture of parental expectations. I have moments of extreme motivation and moments of no motivation at all. I am very goal-oriented. I am hard on myself on a day-to-day basis, and I set high standards of both effort and technical precision. When I trained, I would train at a self-critical level. Being self-critical allowed me to master the technical precision of my sport. Then I would go into a race and I would have a tendency to stay at a self-critical level. Thinking critically is different than thinking negatively. You don't want to think negatively. When your mind is in a state of self-criticism, it becomes very difficult for the body to flow as the mind is always looking for what is wrong. When it comes to actually performing, the mind needs to look for what is right.

A very fundamental shift for me was to be able to use that self-critical mode in training. That helped me progress in a way that was comfortable. I was able to use my natural proclivity of thinking, which was to be hard on myself. Two weeks before a major event, I needed to soften that self-critical voice and shift my mind into a more confident and more self-congratulatory state. So when I went to a race, I would race more to my potential, and my body would be free to flow. That was a turning point for me.

I make the shift very consciously. It is being aware, and being conscious that imagery is something I am controlling. We—all of us—can easily settle into patterns that aren't conscious. You hear that all the time: "Don't think so negatively." When you are in control of your imagery rather than it controlling you, it becomes a tool rather than the enemy. That's the challenge. You have to consciously ask yourself: *What are the effective images? What are the ineffective images? And how are you going to pull yourself around into the effective images at every opportunity?*

Awareness is such an important tool. Be aware of what is constructive and what isn't and have a plan around it. There was a time when I was younger that I would think about sport too much. I was imagining it every moment, and that is too much. Even if it is positive, we need balance in our brain and in our life. So it is about making time and space for imagining. It is about finding the way that is going to work for you. It is about giving time to it, to think about it and picture the detail of it. The more detailed the image, the better it is to conjure and make real. I think self-awareness in life in general, and sport in particular, is very important because it helps you notice the roadblocks you have put in your way. It also lets you notice what you've done really well to get out of your own way.

Today, my focus is on athletes—creating healthy, successful athletes. My purpose is to help people generate their own personal success. I love helping them fulfill their dreams and build happy and healthy relationships in the process. I actively tell athletes what it is that I want them to do. I tell them, "I'm selecting this team. This is what I want you to show." At times they get stuck on what they think is important and don't hear what I am saying. They might think it's important that they paddle 5 kilometres really fast, but I'm saying it's important they show their technical skill and they are committing to the team.

It is one thing to dream something. It's another thing to be aware of the process outside yourself that determines whether you can achieve that dream. So when there is a coach selecting a team, I want athletes to ask themselves, *What is important to that coach specifically, and how do I demonstrate that is something I can do?*

In creating our dream, it's really important not to hold on too tight to what we see as the most important aspect, but to allow ourselves to make sure we are informed by the actual reality of the world and what aspects other people are looking for you to fulfill. This will increase your opportunity and increase their support for you. How do you leverage or use other people you know to inform your own dream versus getting stuck in how you're doing it and what's important to you? There are two kinds of people. There are people who actually make decisions on your success, and there are those who can support you and move you forward toward success. Sometimes they are the same people and sometimes they're different.

As an introvert, it took me a long time to know how to ask for help or where to ask for help rather than doing it all on my own. Having more success made it easier. It was a lot easier to prepare for my second Olympics than it was to prepare for my first because of my faith in myself. Because of this, other people saw my potential and my commitment in a different way.

———

KAMINI BROUGHT TO my attention just how much my mind (well, my thoughts really) did not support me. I started to read about neuroscience and the brain. I would highly recommend Dr. Srinivasan S. Pillay's books if you are interested in learning more about how the brain works. Once I understood how the brain was programmed for survival, I started to very consciously shift my mindset. To use Kamini's words, I shifted my thinking to a more self-congratulatory and supportive state so I could enter the flow of my life. I see flow as an important aspect of a thriving life.

Questions for Self-Reflection

1. Kamini's introversion could have been viewed as a liability. Instead of allowing it to hold her back, she found a sport where her introversion helped her thrive. What characteristic of yours are you perhaps seeing as a liability? What activity could you involve yourself in and thrive by embracing those perceived liabilities?

2. Identify at least three ways where a characteristic that you may see as negative—such as introversion, or critical, outrageous, and quirky views—can actually be viewed as an asset.

3. How do your thoughts and imagery work for you?

4. How could you shift your self-talk to be more supportive of yourself and your goals?

5. As a coach selecting a team, Kamini wants her athletes to ask themselves, *What is important to my coach, and how do I demonstrate that is something I can do?* Who in your life should you be asking, "What is important to you and how can I demonstrate to you I can do that?"

Building Resilience

PADDY TORSNEY

Former Member of Canadian Parliament,
United Nations Permanent Observer, and President
of the Inter-Parliamentary Union

" Dream big. Yes, dream big. "

PADDY TORSNEY IS someone I had always heard about. Her brother and my younger sister went to high school together. My parents knew her quite well because she was their Member of Parliament and attended their church. I met Paddy for the first time at the annual Women's Day Breakfast in Burlington, Ontario. She impressed me as a woman who really had a love for her community and wanted to have a positive impact on the world, which is why I asked to interview her for this book. Paddy has the gift of making people feel seen. Talking to her, I instantly felt I had a friend. There is something about her that creates an immediate feeling that she is there to help and she is on your side.

Paddy is a permanent observer to the United Nations and president of the New York office at the Inter-Parliamentary Union (IPU), which is the international organization of parliaments and the focal point for worldwide parliamentary dialogue. It works for peace, cooperation, and the establishment of representative democracy. Paddy's key focus there is to advance sustainable development and improve democratic governance.

For twelve and a half years, Paddy represented Burlington, Ontario, as a Member of Parliament in the Canadian House of Commons. During her time in office, she was parliamentary secretary to the minister of the environment and later to the minister of international cooperation. She served as deputy principal secretary to Stéphane Dion, leader of the Opposition. Paddy has a bachelor of commerce degree specializing in international business and marketing. She has a public and government relations background. Her volunteer experience includes chair of Burlington's United Way Campaign; host of *The Round Table*, a community affairs program on Cogeco Cable; board member of ROCK: Reach Out Centre for Kids, Halton's children's mental health facility; and a member of the United Way of Burlington and Greater Hamilton Leadership Committee. Paddy is an advocate for women at home and abroad and has hosted an International Women's Day breakfast in Burlington since 1996.

There is an authenticity to Paddy. She loves sharing her story, especially when it will help someone else succeed, and yet she has expectations for those who reach out to her. She wants them to do their research before they meet, she wants to see that they are using the information she provides, and she wants to hear how her advice has been applied.

Paddy learned early in life that if you take small risks and fail, you build resilience. Resilience is built by putting things in perspective—relax, not everyone can be top of the class. It can also be built by speaking to yourself in a reassuring way and by finding people to support you when you feel like you can't get there on your own.

Key messages from Paddy:

- We all stumble. Be resilient and don't put too much pressure on yourself.
- Don't carry too much stuff. It will weigh you down.
- Sometimes it's lonely.
- When you hear, "I can't do this," it may not be true. Give it a try and find out.
- There are angels along the way to help you get to where you're going.
- Take little risks and don't be afraid to stand out.
- Reassure yourself, *Things are going to be okay.*
- Pay it forward.

———————

I WOULDN'T HAVE thought of myself as a dreamer, but I suppose I am. In general, I would like the world to be a place where all of us can achieve our potential, despite the limits imposed upon us. I want to make sure that all girls and boys can pursue whatever they want, not because they are told to but because that is what they want to do. We will have a better world if we are all working to our potential and if gender isn't assigned to certain careers. That way we would get the best teachers, nurses, and engineers. We need to find ways to help people be who they want to be. Maybe as part of a better world, we learn to appreciate each other. I am visualizing a world where we move through the current turmoil to something that is fair and supportive, where we learn to appreciate each other.

As I get older, I realize how important resiliency is and how much we need to help ensure people become more resilient. We need to help ensure people who stumble find a way to work through challenges. We will all have some failure along the way, especially for people who are high achievers. I remember the first time I got a D in school. I was heartbroken. None of it made sense. But there was a great teacher who helped me through it. I figured out partway through university that if I couldn't be at the top of my class—which I clearly wasn't going to be—I didn't have to kill myself trying to be at the top. Do you really need to be an A? Maybe if you are going on to a second degree, but otherwise does anyone ask about grades? When I realized that, it took the pressure off.

More recently I've had a couple friends who have reinforced this need for support and core resilience, as they've crashed into the depths of despair over losses and had a hard time recovering or making a new life plan. I feel fortunate to have been raised in conditions that allowed me to be resilient in the face of loss, to have had family and friends to lean on.

I am generally a very positive person. I like to engage with people, although I have more introverted characteristics than most people would realize, happily spending time alone. My personality publicly and privately is pretty much the same, which I am told makes life easier. I have done some interesting things in my career and I am lucky to have elements of my mother's personality, which includes fighting injustice and not accepting things the way they are just because they have always been that way. To tell me that "it has always been that way" is like holding up a red flag to a bull.

I took a year off between high school and university. I worked two jobs over the summer to travel to Europe with a friend. My godparents lived in Switzerland and every birthday and Christmas I would get a package from them. As a child, I would look at a map of Europe and plan where we would travel when I got older. While I had planned to travel with a friend, she changed her mind and headed to university. So I kept working for the year then travelled alone for three months. When I was ready to leave for Europe, I felt lonely. All my friends were coming home from first-year university and I was leaving for the summer and then heading off to my first year at McGill University when I returned. I remember crying my eyes out on the plane thinking, *What have I done?* I had never even been to summer camp and here I was on a plane to Europe by myself. My first twenty-four hours in Europe were spent waiting for my lost suitcase that had everything in it. But again, it all worked out. Those three months taught me a lot about being alone, working through difficult situations, and relying on the kindness of strangers.

I went to Ireland, spent time in Geneva, and then went to Italy. I arrived at the train station in Florence at five o'clock in the morning and thought, *What am I doing here? I can't do this. I cannot do this. There is no way I can do this.* I had to find a place to stay and was exhausted from half a night's sleep. My plan was to wait until it was eight o'clock and places opened. As I sat there, worried, I kept thinking, *I can't do this.* Then I noticed a woman sitting behind and thought she looked Canadian. I don't know why. So I flashed the Canadian flag that was on my purse and held up my English book. All of a sudden she turned around and asked me, "Hey, do you speak English?" I looked at her and said, "Oh, my God, you're from McGill University. You gave me the campus tour last month." Needless to say, it was a wonderful surprise to meet this Canadian, a seasoned traveller who could speak some Italian, and we decided to share a room in a *pensione*, a small hotel. She was really helpful, getting me oriented and encouraging me to send half the stuff in my backpack back to Geneva. And she was right. Even after cutting back, I still had too much stuff.

Then I got to Siena, my next stop, by myself and asked myself again, *Okay, what do I do now?* I started to look around and I realized that every *pensione* was over $100/night and I couldn't afford that on my $25/day travel budget. Getting disheartened, I turned around when a man called, "Hey, Miss Canada." It was a man I had spoken with from the train. He was from Prince Rupert, BC. He took pity on me, walking me around and negotiating to find me a place that was affordable, like $12. I felt I had angels help me to find my way. Now, every day in New York or elsewhere, when I see people on the street corner looking confused, I always ask if they need help. I think of the people who helped me. Sometimes I even meet some really interesting people that way. It feels good to put someone on the right path. Life is more fulfilling when you bump into people.

On that same trip to Europe, in Munich, Germany, after buying too many Picasso posters at an exhibit, I scrimped on dinner. The result: I got a severe case of food poisoning. In the middle of the night, alone in a large youth hostel bathroom crying and barfing, I started to choke. I remember thinking, *NO! You must get through this. It's a horrible place to die, alone.* I was nineteen years old, so the drama is fair. I kept reassuring myself, *I'll get through this. It feels awful but I will get through this.* I negotiated finding a doctor, getting drugs, and staying in bed to sleep it off. Alone and sick with no options, I talked myself through the episode. I realized if I called my parents there was nothing they could do except worry and I didn't want that. I waited until I was in Copenhagen and feeling better to call them. I guess the key lesson was to take a little risk, expand your horizons, and things will be okay. You might even meet someone interesting. Travelling, taking calculated risks, and learning to test yourself—especially early in life—can open up lots of opportunities.

My parents taught me the art of "looking like you belong" when we went to the Olympics in 1976. "Go and take those better seats until someone else comes along and tells you to get out of the chair." So they reinforced the message "Don't be afraid to stand out, it is not embarrassing. Don't be afraid to go for the things you want," and I suppose that carried through all the way to "Don't be afraid to put your name on the ballot." I did just that. Somebody asked me to think about running to be a Member of Parliament (MP) when I was twenty-nine, just as I was headed to France. My first reaction was, "No, that's ridiculous. I'm twenty-nine and that's an impossible task." I decided to stay focused on going to France for the month so I could figure out what I wanted to do next. At the time, I was working in my second job out of university and I wasn't particularly happy. I needed to get away and learn French and try to retract things. I told myself that I was absolutely not going to think about running as a candidate while I was gone. Of course my mind still worked subconsciously. As the month went on I started to think about it more. I began role-playing it in my head. Even today, when I think about my next move, I try to imagine myself taking that step, being in that place or having that job. I often tell people who are trying to figure out their next steps: "Just imagine what your life would look like if you make those choices."

I imagined what it would be like to be an MP. There were few real examples for me. When I ran, MPs were mostly older men. I knew some of the members of Ontario's provincial Parliament because I had worked there. I tested the idea with a couple of trusted friends and received positive responses with clear offers to help. I began believing that it wasn't out of the realm of possibility for me to run. I believed there needed to be more women representatives in Parliament, more young people, and that helped to compel me to run as a candidate. Being an MP, chair of the Women's Caucus, and a member of the Justice Committee at a particularly intense time in Canadian history, the first two years were a blur.

After two years as an MP in Ottawa, one of my friends was visiting Ottawa at Christmas, when Parliament Hill is particularly beautiful. The hallways are lined with trees with red bows and white lights. My friend kept saying, "You work here. You work here!" I was like, "I know, isn't it crazy?" It was a wonderful reminder of how special a place it was to work, and how important the work we were doing was. I spent twelve years in Parliament.

I was encouraged to run, and now that is something I pay forward. When people with a certain eagerness in their eyes say, "Tell me about the first time you ran," I say, "You want to run? Have you thought about running?" I get serious. I advise them to get their friends and family on board and tell them to think about what it would be like to have the job. It is possible at any age.

———

PADDY INSPIRED ME to read about self-compassion, which was not something I had learned in my life. Her ability to calm herself with reassuring words intrigued me. When I searched *self-compassion* on the web, I found Dr. Kristin Neff, a self-compassion researcher who advocates doing exactly what Paddy innately does to soothe herself in difficult situations. I now use comforting words to soothe myself when I feel challenged and it works!

Questions for Self-Reflection

1. Sitting in a train station in Florence, Paddy said to herself over and over, *I can't do this,* and yet by being open to connecting with others she did it. When have you overcome the thought *I can't do this*? What steps did you take in order to overcome this thought?

2. Suffering food poisoning in Germany, Paddy reassured herself that she would get through it. How do you reassure yourself when you are struggling? What compassionate words could you use to reassure yourself?

3. Throughout her travels in Europe, Paddy was unexpectedly helped along the way. When have you been unexpectedly helped along the way?

4. Paddy pays it forward. She remembers the help she received from strangers when travelling in Europe as a young woman and seeks to help others in the same way. She also encourages people to get into politics, just like she was encouraged by others. How have you paid it forward? How could you pay it forward?

5. As Paddy was making the decision about whether to become a Member of Parliament, she imagined herself there and asked a few trusted friends their thoughts, and she realized it was not out of the realm of possibility. What could you imagine yourself doing? Take some time and really put yourself there. What does it look like? Make it as real as you can. If it is something you really want to happen, take time every day and visualize it happening. Live from the feeling that you are already there.

Professional Rabble-Rouser

JANE HANLON

Professional Rabble-Rouser, Founder of
Greening Niagara, and Mother

66 *Don't wait for somebody else to do what you see needs doing.* 99

I HAVE KNOWN JANE Hanlon for many years. We both worked in the environmental field and so ran into each other a lot at public consultation events. We came from different perspectives—mine the perspective of industry and hers the perspective of a grassroots activist. She was not always liked and yet she was able to create change. I see Jane as an ardent fighter for the environment. It is Jane's nature to research, and as a result she knows a lot about the science of climate change. Her passion led her to create an environmental action network. We met at a vegan café. I noticed that Jane spoke her mind and did not hesitate to correct me if I had misunderstood what she was saying.

With a lifelong dedication to environmental issues, Jane was the founding executive director of Climate Action Niagara, which was later rebranded as Greening Niagara, a grassroots environmental organization in the Niagara region. Greening Niagara focused on eco-education in action and provided tools for people to make lifestyle changes that support the community and the environment.

Jane developed and led educational programs including urban greening, community gardening, food security workshops, tours of renewable energy projects, workshops for active transit, and land use planning. She also introduced Eco-Fest Niagara, a celebration of all things greener and cleaner. With an education in business, horticulture, and soil science, she has been involved in conservation for many years. She was the owner/operator of Gardens by Design, an ecologically sound landscaping company that specialized in slope retention and soils restoration.

Also involved with the Niagara Children's Centre, Jane provided children's veggie-growing workshops, developed and trained adult gardening crews, and assisted with workshops on propagation. Her volunteer activities include president of the Niagara District Council of Women, a board member of Land Care Niagara, and a member of the Regional Niagara Waste Advisory Committee, Biochar Ontario, Ontario Urban Forest Council, Environmental Defence, Ontario Greenbelt Alliance, DSBN High Skills ENERGY, Council of Canadians, Sustainability Network of Ontario, and Ontario Sustainable Energy

Association. Jane is now retired and focusing her efforts on creating an eco-retreat centre in Northern Ontario.

The effect of carbon emissions on the biodiversity of the planet is one of her going concerns. She is devoted to raising awareness about the catastrophic dangers of climate instability and teaching people simple steps they can take to better support the environment. She was raised in a time when the environment was not on the world stage. It required a strong voice and persistence to be on the agenda.

In order to create Climate Action Niagara, Jane had to overcome seeing her introversion as an impediment and take the lead. Her childhood prepared her well for grassroots environmental action. She was surrounded by social justice activists who were making a difference. She learned how to be a caretaker of the soil, how to grow fruits and vegetables, and how to preserve them so she could eat local foods year-round. She made a career of sharing the skills she learned with others.

Key messages from Jane:

- If there is something that you think needs to change, don't look around for someone else to do it. Take the lead.
- Don't be afraid to put your foot in your mouth now and again.
- Don't get hung up on making things perfect.
- Laugh at yourself.
- If role models don't show up in your everyday life, go out and find role models.
- Make a list of who can help you, then ask for their help.
- Make a plan and go out, take action, and make it happen.

———

I AM A professional rabble-rouser. I was not that well-behaved executive director one would expect. I don't know if I actually rabble-rouse. Maybe I simply give people an opportunity to follow what they want to do. I'm an introvert. Leading an organization was not what I really intended to do. I would rather be in my backyard, thank you very much. I just got tired of waiting for someone else to take the actions that I so clearly saw needed to be taken. So I stepped up to make them happen. When I first started speaking in public, I quivered at the knees. I could barely be heard. In order to get the job done, I had to get over that. You get used to saying stupid things. Every now and then the foot is in the mouth. You need a sense of humour. I can't imagine doing anything else, so this is where I am supposed to be. I am honouring it. If you are not following your own journey, you just struggle that much more.

There are so many opportunities to make a difference, even in small ways, and they all add up. Just start. When we first had a vision that we wanted to create an organization, we began talking to others. The one main refrain that kept coming back to us was, "I wish I knew what to do." Our response: There were a million things to do. People kept telling us to list them, to start writing them down. I was able to draw on people from almost every environmental organization in Niagara. I would think this person could do that and I would just go and ask them to do what they were good at. More brass than you know.

I have been working on environmental issues since I was a child. I think people choose their path at a very early age, maybe five or six years old. My first act as an activist was at age eleven. I removed election signs that had been nailed to trees and marched them back to the respective campaign headquarters and told them they could not do that and gave them a lesson in caring for the environment. I was raised to question data, information, and assumption, which in turn led me to question authority and may have been interpreted as a disrespect for authority. You know, "Are you kidding me? Please justify that." I am not sure at what point that kicked in.

My father was a man of few words. He was very warm, very kind, and a little shell-shocked from the war. He wouldn't tell me stories, he would hand me an apple and say, "Smell this." I remember sitting on his lap when he played the guitar and feeling the vibration of the instrument and his legs thumping and his arms flailing. He had a curiosity about just about everything to do with the planet, from watercourses [lakes, rivers, and streams] to making our own soap. Of course, the soap he made would rot our skin off. I remember he brought some goslings home and didn't know where to put them. First they went in the closet and ruined my mother's clothes... that didn't go over well. They then went into the bathtub and then to a pool in the backyard, and then he couldn't kill them for food so they went off to a farm.

My childhood house was like *Green Acres* [a TV sitcom about an urban couple who moved from New York City to a farm in the country]. My mother was city and my father was country. She was Scottish. He was Irish. It was a rowdy household. My father liked to grow food. Canning was the norm, as well as composting. He was always paying attention to the soil. Healthy soil is rich in nutrients, fibre, and microbial diversity. If that wasn't right, then you'd messed up. I learned a lot about soil health from my father. We had kittens and our earliest lesson from my father was, "What does it want?" So not knowing it, he taught respect for other species. My parents hosted refugees who came to Canada. We taught them the fine points of how to use coins, where the stores were, how to turn on a washing machine, and that just because water is ever-flowing doesn't mean you flow it forever. At the dinner table we always had extras. When we had visitors at the door, my father would yell, "Put another potato on."

At the dinner table, all topics were discussed. There was no hiding the good, the bad, and the ugly; it was all there. We were quite welcome in the conversation as long as we had something to add. So we needed to come up to their level—talk like adults.

If you wanted to join the conversation on any given day, you were expected to have read at least two or three newspapers and be able to speak from different perspectives. My mother's hobby was to clip newspaper articles and keep files pertaining to transportation, food, urban structure, urban planning, soil capacity, and all of those wonderful things.

My parents provided a rich background for me. They were part of an organization called World Wise. They were members of Healthy Cities and PALS [Preservation of Agricultural Lands Society], both of which were born and bred in my parents' living room, and of course the Council of Women. I remember Gracia Janes, Margherita Howe, Laura Sabia—amazing activists who made a difference in the world. Social activism comes from feeling a sense of social responsibility, and my parents instilled this in me.

I was a landscape designer. When I wanted to determine what was healthy and what was not, what could be salvaged, what could not, it was a sense of touch that I would use to know if something was alive. Even before you take your nail and peel back the bark and see, you know. It was the temperature coursing through it.

A big turning point for me was when my son asked me to visit because he wanted to discuss the documentary *An Inconvenient Truth*. He had seen it before it became the film that we all know. When it was first released, it had a three-day run so there was not a lot of media hype. What the media did report was that it was a lousy movie and it was dismissed. My son played it for me. I found it so disturbing, so rattling, because I recalled newspaper articles that told us about the issues in the 1960s and 1970s. I remember the data Al Gore first brought to the U.S. Congress and the splash that it made at the time. How on earth could we have let it go—not sitting up, not measuring, not paying attention? All this time and now we are in this state of "Oh My God." I had to have my son turn the movie off five, six, seven times while I just paced and paced and held my stomach and breathed deeply. I kept coming back to it because I had to get through it. I had to see it. It was at that point that I realized I could no longer turn a blind eye. How are we going to solve the problem if we can't look at it?

It brought me to the space of—what am I going to do? I can't deal with this. I don't know this. Who does know this? I started jotting names down about who could help and how. For three years, I spent half of each day researching about climate change. I was physically and mentally unprepared by what I was reading. I found this website that consolidated environmental articles from media around the world. What I was reading shocked me to my core. At times, I just put a halt to my researching while I found my feet again. Everything I read fed my plans and actions for change. If you have a serious concern and you are worried about something, then create a plan of action and go out and make it happen. Don't wait for somebody else to do what you see needs doing.

———————

WHAT I LEARNED from Jane is if I am passionate about making something happen, it's important to let go of perfection and just do it imperfectly. I am becoming aware of how my need for perfection delays so many of my ideas from manifesting. Nothing in nature is perfect, yet it is incredibly effective in its imperfection.

Questions for Self-Reflection

1. Jane's childhood taught her all the things she needed to co-create Greening Niagara: social responsibility, activism, how to grow her own food, and how to make it last, as well as the importance of being informed and speaking her mind. How has your childhood prepared you to create in the world?

2. As a child, Jane had several grassroots social justice and environmental activists organizing in her living room, who were her role

models. Jane witnessed how the work of those activists made a difference and changed society for the better. Who were your role models in childhood? What did your role models teach you?

3. Who are your roles models today and what are they teaching you?

4. The film *An Inconvenient Truth* had an impact on Jane. What movie(s) moved you, or made you feel the need to take action or make change in your life?

5. Combatting climate change became one of Jane's causes. What issue, challenge, or cause moves you?

It's Not Just About Money

JODY STEINHAUER

Chief Bargain Officer, the Bargains Group;
Founder, Engage and Change; and Mother

> 66 *I truly believe that everyone is on this earth for a reason, a purpose, and you need to figure out what that is.* 99

JODY STEINHAUER IS a passionate entrepreneur with a commitment to helping others. She is very clear about who she is and what's important to her, and makes her business decisions based on that. She shifted the vision for her company when she realized how much more rewarding it was to work with not-for-profits than large retailers. I was so impressed with how Jody has navigated her own life from a very young age. She understands the power of networking and has used it in both her professional and personal evolution.

Jody is the founder, president, and chief bargain officer of the Bargains Group, an award-winning, multimillion-dollar discount wholesaler. As chief bargain officer, she uses her network and buying power to help companies and not-for-profit agencies maximize their buying dollar. She lives by the philosophy "giving back makes great business sense" and runs the Bargains Group and national charity Engage and Change from that mindset. Engage and Change inspires people and businesses to engage in a hands-on experience with a tangible outcome that will change the daily lives of people in her communities. Project Water and

Project Winter Survival are initiatives spearheaded by Engage and Change. They provide frontline relief with summer survival kits, including bottled water, and winter survival kits, complete with a sleeping bag. Jody gives back as a mentor and motivational speaker, sharing her business philosophy and expertise to help others grow themselves, their businesses, and their skills and knowledge about helping others.

Jody is the recipient of numerous honours, including the Rotman Canadian Woman Entrepreneur of the Year, Canada's Top 40 under 40, the Board of Trade's Business Leader of the Year Award, the Business Excellence Award in the Community, the Humanitarian of the Year Award, Canada's Profit W100 Award, and many others.

Jody is a unique, genuine, and caring leader who views everything in her life as an opportunity. She is clear about her boundaries and not afraid to articulate them. Her confident, assertive style can be a challenge for some. Her idol is Wonder Woman, and an image of Wonder Woman hangs on Jody's wall. On challenging days in the office, she wears her Wonder Woman belt to lighten the mood and make her team laugh. Jody's business shifted when she let go of what a business was supposed to be and started making business decisions that aligned with her values.

Key messages from Jody:

- Make conscious choices that align with who you are.
- Be clear about who you are and what you are not willing to put up with.
- Define what success looks like to you.
- Be a sponge for learning.
- Shift your perspective to see challenges as opportunities.
- Ask for help—it shows strength.
- Giving back makes good business sense.

———

THERE IS NO company like mine. The Bargains Group has come out of my passion for identifying and constantly making choices about my boundaries. If I don't like it and if it doesn't look good to me, or make me feel good, then I don't do it. I made a huge choice years ago. I decided that I didn't want to work with retail stores because it wasn't fun. It is so much more rewarding to work with the Salvation Army than some of the retail buyers who yelled and screamed at me while ignoring my phone calls and not paying their bills. Although these businesses were very lucrative for me, I made the choice to not make them the focus of my business. I said to myself, *If I'm going to work this hard, I want to work with people who respect me. I want to make an impact and help people and feel good about it.* There are benefits on all sides. This was a conscious choice. I make it consistently when I make my daily business decisions. I am very clear on who I am, what my beliefs are, what my brand is. Those are my filters. If anything is going to get in the way or potentially cloud my beliefs, my brand, or who I am, then that is the wrong decision to make, the wrong path to go down.

I'm a very positive, outgoing, and creative individual. I am in touch with who I am and what I want in my life. Every day, I'm constantly figuring out how I am going to get there. What is important to me is how I can make it better for others who are important to me. I'm a very confident, assertive woman, a definite leader. I have a positive attitude about everything that happens to me no matter how black it could be. I look at everything in life as an opportunity and I'm a sponge for learning. I'm very transparent. I will respectfully say it like it is—let's cut to the chase. I am proactive and very realistic. I am comfortable with who I am.

I had an epiphany that changed the direction of the company. I met a woman who worked in a homeless shelter. When I found out what she did for a living, and she found out what I did, I realized I could have a massive impact on the homeless by providing desperately needed items at huge discounts. This was an epiphany because I realized, wow, not only is it really powerful from a business perspective, but it feels good. What a rewarding situation to have your client thank you, hug you, and tell you that you've made a difference. I really understood the impact I was having when a client told me that she gained an incredible amount of confidence from the fresh, clean pair of underwear I provided her for a job interview. To see clients go to interviews feeling better about themselves—and it's obvious in their body language, posture, and the way they speak—all because of the things that I helped to drive. That's amazing. That is success for me. I always tell people to figure out what success looks like and then just work backwards. If you don't know what success looks like, then ask the person who is defining it. If someone is giving you a project to do and you don't know what an A+ looks like, then that is your fault. Ask what it looks like. I say to my kids all the time, ask your teacher what is 100 percent. If you know what it looks like, then it is much easier to obtain.

I am blessed. I love shopping. I love clothing, on a very superfi-
cial basis, I love feeling and looking good and I love to help people.
I built this incredible company where I get to shop for a living and
make people happy by giving them great bargains and solutions
that are creative and out of the box. I have a division of the company that is focused specifically on those in need.

All my life I have taken paths that most would never take. I'm
asked why I put so much effort into helping the homeless. "Why
not focus on making money?" For me it comes down to the
360-degree picture. It is not just about money and it's not just
about accomplishing this or that. It is about the feeling that comes
from the accomplishment. Helping people. Helping them find solutions and remove barriers inspires me. People inspire me. If people
are passionate and have a vision and dream that I am attracted to, I
sit there, listen, and try to absorb as much as I can. Then I take out
the best parts of what they have said and I apply that to my life. I
wanted to be the best mother I could. I looked around and asked,
"Who could be my role model? Who do I look up to? Who am I going
to model my behaviour after?"

I try to motivate people to be more outward, to look to others
who need help rather than constantly focusing on themselves. I've
created a charity, Engage and Change, to facilitate people working
together and help them use their skill sets and their passions to
make a difference in their communities. There is so much need and
so many people who truly want to help and don't know how. I like
to bring this together. I would like it to be the norm that everyone
who runs a company has the belief that they should give some of
their time and encourage their employees to give of their time to
help the not-for-profit sector. It's not about writing a cheque. It's
about the huge amount of benefit that an individual or company
can have by applying its skills and leveraging others to do the same
thing. We have a lot of problems in society and we have to learn to
fix them. As business people, we are great at removing obstacles

and solving problems, so why not apply those skill sets to the not-for-profit sector and teach them how we do it?

I never think that things aren't working. They may just not be working at the optimal level. I evaluate the situation. What must happen in order for it to work? Who can help? I've built a huge network of people, but they can't help me if I am not able to identify what I need help with. Asking for help is a huge tool that a lot of people don't use. I encourage people around me to ask for help. People seem to have been trained to view asking for help as a weakness. Asking for help is a strength. Why would you struggle when all around you are people who want to help? Why not ask?

The first half of my life has been about how to do, who I am, and what I want. Now that I have figured this out, the second half is going to be: How can I leverage all of this to change the universe? I'm about helping. That's my constant. I ask myself, *How can I make everything wow for everybody?* That is what motivates me, knowing that I helped and had an impact in some way, on some level.

———

THE IMPORTANCE OF asking for help was the gift Jody gave me. Why struggle when I can just ask for help? Asking for help is definitely not second nature to me. Offering help is more my style. It seems to be a huge chasm for me, moving from offering to asking for help, and I practise jumping that chasm daily. I remind myself every day that asking for help implies strength.

Questions for Self-Reflection

1. Jody describes herself as a confident, assertive leader who is very positive, outgoing, and creative. How do you describe yourself?

2. Jody's philosophy is "giving back makes great business sense." What is the philosophy you want to live by?

3. In order to do well, Jody ensures she knows what success looks like, what an A+ looks like. What project are you working on right now that knowing what A+ looks like would help you succeed on? Who can you ask to find out?

4. Asking for help is something Jody knows how to do. She also expects her employees to ask for help when they need it. What do you need help with right now? Who could you ask to get the help you need?

5. Before Jody aligned her business to her philosophy, it wasn't fun dealing with large retailers. She felt disrespected. How do you feel when your choices aren't aligned with who you are?

6. Jody believes it is not just about making money and it's not about accomplishing this or that. It is about how you feel about what you accomplish. What is the feeling you want from your accomplishments? What would you be doing differently if you focused on the feeling you want from your accomplishments?

You Can Always
Be an Entrepreneur

SHEENA REPATH

Cofounder and Chief Inspirer of Making
Sh*t Happen at MSH District

> *It isn't circumstances which give you opportunities. It is your ability to have big ideas, to have dreams and to then know how to go out and go after them.*

I AM SO GRATEFUL for the enthusiasm and support Sheena Repath provided me throughout the creation of this book. Without her, it would have taken me a lot longer than it did. She generously connected me to her network of amazing women, several of whom are included in this book. I met Sheena at a Women in Leadership Conference that my niece Sarah organized for the York University Business School. Sheena spoke before me. While I was listening to her, I thought, *I have to interview this woman!* and I am so glad that I did. We met over lunch at a very busy Italian bistro.

Sheena makes sh*t happen. She helps people bring their dreams, ideas, and products to life. She has ten years of professional experience as a designer, entrepreneur, and adviser in the fashion/apparel industry. Her expertise ranges from concept creation, design, product development, and manufacturing to wholesale, retail, and online distribution. She started Ideal Samples Inc. in 2008 to fill a growing need in the marketplace for individuals and businesses that have ideas or concepts but need samples or products or help bringing them to market. Sheena and her team of experts have worked on hundreds of ideas and products for such leading brands as Indian Motorcycle, American Brands, Asics, The Answer, and V.

Sheena is a vivacious, confident woman. There is an ease to her that suggests she trusts that the universe is on her side. Her enthusiasm and zest for life are contagious. Sheena has enough energy to ignite the world into greatness. She dreams big, creates a plan to get there, engages people who can advocate for her, and then takes the first small step to get started. She tried a few things out before she found her place as an entrepreneur and wasn't afraid to change directions. When her college teacher told her, "You just process differently," Sheena was able to give up believing that her way was wrong and realized there are always other ways to do things.

Key messages from Sheena:

- Don't worry. No matter how daunting it looks, start where you are and plan your way forward.
- Sometimes what we think we want isn't quite what we thought it would be. There is no harm in giving it a try and finding out.
- Take actions toward what you want.

- Don't be afraid to change direction.
- There is no right way to think and no right way to be. Be yourself. It is easiest.
- Find someone to advocate for you, to guide you.
- Drive your own life, even when people may not agree with your direction.

———

I WAS A terrible student. I wasn't very smart. I just grazed through every class. My guidance counsellor and teachers were always pushing my dad to let me take general courses in the less-intensive class. He was like, "No, no, no. I don't want there to be any disadvantage in her life. She is going to have to work. I don't care if she gets 50 percent. She is going through it and will be okay." After these meetings, I would be fearful that I would be in trouble and my dad kept saying, "Don't worry. You are going to be an entrepreneur." And I'm like, "What? I don't even know what that means."

In high school, I was failing miserably. My dad would say, "We are going to get you a tutor. Don't worry, you are going to be an entrepreneur." And I am thinking, *Dad, entrepreneurs need ideas. I don't even have an idea.* And he planted the seed again, "Don't worry. Go out and try a whole bunch of things. Don't worry because you are going to be an entrepreneur."

In grade eleven, I decided what I wanted to do. I went home and told my dad that I knew what I wanted to be when I grew up. "I want to be a pediatric surgeon," I said. And the look on his face was *Are you kidding me? You have seen your grades, right?* But what he said was, "Okay, make an appointment with the guidance counsellor. Let's go in. Let's talk to them." So I picked an idea. I hated sciences. I hated all that stuff. Who knows where it came from, but we had built a dialogue together that allowed me to go to my dad with any idea. He would always empower me to explore it.

So we go into the guidance counsellor's office and sit down. I tell the counsellor I want to be a pediatric surgeon, and the guidance counsellor was like, "You've got to be kidding me." But my dad insisted, "We know where we're at in terms of academics, so what do we do?" And the guidance counsellor said, "It's eighteen years of schooling. Sheena is going to have to go to university. She doesn't have the grades." And my dad strikes back with, "I didn't ask you if it's possible. I want to know how we get started. She wants to do this, so we are doing it." And the counsellor went on again, "It's university and she doesn't have the sciences and her English is horrendous." And Dad said, "I'm only going to say it one more time. We understand. We're aware of the situation. How do we get started?" The counsellor responded, "Great. She needs to go to college and she needs to take basic nursing and she is going to have to take remedial math and English because her grades are so horrendous." My dad said, "Great, okay, pick three colleges that you want to go to and let's apply."

I got into the program. I had to take remedial everything and the first quarter of school I was an A+ student. The dean of the program actually pulled me aside and was like, "We are a bit concerned. Was something going on in school? Your transcripts from here and from high school are very different." "No," I responded, "I just love what I'm learning. I just love it." They just laughed, and it was my first realization that we are all in control of making decisions. Whether it was the right decision, whether I was going to be a pediatric surgeon or a nurse of something in between, it didn't matter. I had an idea. Someone around me helped me explore how to get started and I took action.

In my first placement, I worked in a seniors' home. I was devastated that they needed me to separate my personal feeling and connections with patients from my work. It was really tough because I was trying to visit my patients on weekends and I was told, "We have ethical standards and you are not allowed to do this." I'm like, "But they don't have family." And they were like, "It doesn't matter. It happens. Monday to Friday stays here and then you go home and have your life." I was appalled and I thought, *I can't separate myself quite like that.* I went home and explained that to my dad and he's like, "Okay, what do you want to do?" I said, "I think I am going to quit and I'm going to work for a bit and I'll figure out what's next."

Looking back now, it was this process that empowered me to have my own ideas, to share them with people, to figure out a game plan and go after them. Did we know it was going to be a painful road? Absolutely. Did we know it was probably not going to be possible? Probably. But why not start? Why not try? What I am finding out is a lot of people don't have that. They are afraid of ideas. They are afraid to try. They simply don't have the support they need to explore.

My second round of college was fashion design. Supportive as always, my dad proclaimed, "You are so *not* taking fashion." And I said, "I love being creative and I love making things. And that has become really clear to me especially after my summer working with you to relaunch the Indian Motorcycle brand [Sheena's father is an entrepreneur and business growth specialist]." I set out and signed up for a program out of town and started fashion design in the fall.

In first year, I had a creative class. *Did they really want to teach us creativity?* I wondered. They taught us so much more than creativity. Wendy Sperry taught my creative class. She changed my life. We were sitting in class one day and she wrote a sequence of numbers on the board and asked us to come up with the next five numbers. Everybody put their head down and went about their business. She then asked for volunteers to put the remaining numbers in the sequence on the board. A classmate went up and completed the number sequence. I was really proud of myself because I got the same numbers. Wendy then asked the girl to explain how she came up with the numbers.

As the girl started to explain, I started to sweat and feel nervous. I thought I was going to throw up because that was not how I got the numbers. Years of being a terrible student came flooding back and I thought, *Here I am again.* I was panicked and Wendy came over and asked, "Did you not get the numbers?" I said, "I got the numbers." And she is like, "Did you get them a different way?" I was so panicked that I had done it wrong that I was having a physical reaction. "Yah, I got it. That's not how I got it." "Well," she said, "Come up. There is not just one way of doing things. Come and explain to me how you got the numbers." So I went up and explained and she is like, "Well, it's right. You obviously got the numbers right. Who else did it that way?" There was one kid, he was like, "That's how I did it." And Wendy responded, "You just process differently." Finally, I could take a deep breath. It was like she gave me permission for the rest of my life. I'm not wrong. There isn't just one way. Wow! There are other ways of doing things. It was one of those times in my life where someone gave me permission to just be me. So now when I am doing things and someone doesn't understand what I am saying, how I did something, or how I see things, I feel I can explain myself instead of it just being wrong or right.

I have ideas, lots of ideas, and ideas are a form of dreaming. Dreaming is a way to drive myself. I don't know where I'm going, I don't have a title or role, or a sum of money. Dreaming allows me to kind of set a benchmark out in the distance and it also allows me to test myself. I conjure up an idealistic way that I see the world or my life being and I can create it. It is me who is driving my life, not society, nor other people's ideas of what my life should look like. If you don't have a dream or vision, then you aren't going anywhere. I use dreaming for everything. I use it to push myself, to inspire other people. My dream is to change the education system. I don't know what that looks like or how it will happen. I want to inspire people. I want people to know anything is possible.

What I put out into the world is what I want in return, so the more I focus on abundance, happiness, great people, great experiences, and adventure, the more I'm going to get in return. I get up and it's like the sun is shining every day.

―――――

SHEENA'S STORY REINFORCES to me the importance of supporting others in their dreams, allowing them to give it a try, no matter how wacky it may seem to me based on what I know of them. There are no mistakes in life, just lessons to harvest our future from. Sheena was also a model for me of how much people are willing to do to support me in creating the next expression of myself.

Questions for Self-Reflection

1. The process of mapping out a route to become a pediatric surgeon was empowering to Sheena. It made her realize if she had an idea, she could figure out a game plan and give it a try. What idea do you have right now, that thing that really appeals to you and yet seems so daunting? How can you get started moving the idea forward? What is one baby step you can take to move forward? Sheena's step was to speak with her guidance counsellor.

2. Who could help you to get there? Sheena had her dad and her guidance counsellor. It doesn't have to be someone close to you. It could be a complete stranger. No matter who they are, just contact them and ask for help. The worst thing that can happen is that they say no. Then you can ask someone else.

3. Sheena didn't let the fact you are supposed to have good grades to be a pediatric surgeon get in her way of finding a path toward that goal. What supposed-to could be holding you back?

4. It changed her life when Sheena's teacher told her, "You just process differently." Before this point, Sheena believed that her thought process was wrong. She has since learned that thinking differently is an asset. What might you believe is wrong about yourself that may just not be true?

5. Sheena now uses what she learned to help others make sh*t happen. Who could you help move forward with their dream?

Sitting on a Park Bench in New York City

JANET NEZON

Nutritionist, Educator, Creator of
Rainbow Plate, Wife, and Mother

> *We really have to listen to our dreams, see them, and allow them to guide us, allow them to teach us things, allow them to shape what we are working toward.*

JANET NEZON HAD a long career before stepping into her dream. I interviewed her over the phone just after she met with Sick Kids Hospital in Toronto, Ontario, and was so excited about the possibilities of collaborating with them. It was such an honour to share the excitement of possibility with her, which has since become a reality.

Janet is the founder of Rainbow Plate: Healthy Eating Made Simple. Rainbow Plate is a not-for-profit educational foundation that provides hands-on solutions to the long-term health of children in Canada. Janet has a bachelor of science degree in nutritional science and a master of health science degree specializing in health promotion. For years, Janet was an academic instructor teaching the science of nutrition.

It was while on a park bench in New York City that Janet had the realization that people don't need more nutrition information. What they do need are simple concepts they can put into action to get back to enjoying food. From this, Rainbow Plate was born. It is now the Rainbow Food Education Foundation. Using Janet's simple and colourful approach to eating well, the foundation inspires children in schools, child-care centres, and camps, as well as health-care and community organizations, to develop a lifelong healthy relationship with food. In addition to her work with children, Janet conducts workshops for parents and educators, inspires people through her speaking engagements, and works as a consultant to help design food education workshops and strategies for her clients.

Being accelerated through school left Janet feeling like she did not fit in. She found her peer group when she was able to say, "This is me." It was listening to a lecturer talk about teaching people in schools about healthy eating that Janet realized, *That's what I want to do*. She created Rainbow Plate thirty years later. When she starts talking about Rainbow Plate, she lights up in a way that only someone who is doing what they love can do. Janet took a risk by letting go of the security of a full-time job as an academic lecturer to create her own business in health promotion. She let go of what she felt health education was supposed to be and discovered a clear and fun way to inspire people of all ages to eat well.

Key messages from Janet:

- At times we all have a feeling we don't fit in.
- Come to terms with who you are, to be able to say, "This is me."
- Follow your passion.
- Sit quietly and you can be inspired.
- Listen to your dreams, see them, and allow them to unfold in their own time.
- When you are ready, focus on your dream and find out if it will fly.
- Embrace the journey—every piece contributes to who you are.
- Find the people who will support your journey.

———

NATURE INSPIRES ME. It sounds ridiculous, but vegetables and fruit inspire me. A lot of what I do is getting kids and adults excited and passionate about fruits and vegetables. Have you ever cut open a purple cabbage and looked at the inside? It is breathtaking. My poor husband will travel along beside me as we go to farmers' markets with my camera as I capture the most incredibly beautiful images, shapes, textures. The colours in nature inspire me.

I'm dreaming of a world that is vibrant and healthy, a world where we are no longer battling the diseases and chronic conditions with which we are currently plagued. This world includes access to those things that promote health, where kids are active, eating healthy foods, and families are sitting down sharing time and food together. In some ways, this world goes back in time. I am working to promote part of that bigger picture.

I was one of those kids who didn't always fit in. I was in the gifted program, one of those kids who got accelerated through the system. I was advanced from grade two to grade three. I remember clearly not fitting in. Socially, I wasn't always so comfortable.

I did not fit in with the grade twos any longer and I didn't fit in with the grade threes. I felt a bit different from some of the kids. I remember wishing I wasn't smart. I had a teacher in grade six who actually sat me down and said, "You know, you are different. You are special. You have something to contribute. You are going to do things." I remember being a bit freaked out by it. At that age, you don't really want to be special. Then I found a peer group. I think a lot of it was coming to terms with who I was and being able to say, "This is me." I found like-minded people. My childhood was happy and comfortable, but interwoven with the challenges of being special or different and not always feeling like that was a good thing.

I am currently pursuing what I have been envisioning for years and years. I am so blessed. My husband is the most amazing cheerleader and supporter. There is no question that I wouldn't be pursuing what I am doing if he had not said, "This is your dream and your vision and if you don't give up everything to focus on it full-time, then you are never going to know if it is going to fly." We really have to listen to those dreams and see them and allow them to guide us and allow them to teach us. We must allow them to help shape what we are working toward.

I was studying nutrition. I had never planned to make nutrition a career in the traditional sense. I was hoping to apply to medical school because I was always fascinated with the human body. I remember being in a fourth-year undergraduate nutritional science class listening to a lecture. Someone had come in and talked about a program that they developed to teach people in schools about healthy eating. I remember looking up and saying, "That's what I want to do!" I remember thinking that I didn't want to be a dietician and this was speaking to me, this notion of motivating others to be excited about being healthy. The professor actually said to me, "You should pursue a degree in health promotion which will teach you about how to do that." That was the first moment of crystallization for me.

Fast-forward thirty years. I am an academic lecturer, a nutritional science health professional. For my birthday in 2006, I asked to go to a conference in the United States. The conference was filled with all the top lecturers in the field of nutrition. It was an opportunity for me to confirm whether I was up to date with the state of nutritional science. I headed to New York City. The conference was very clinical. I remember sitting there and thinking, *Okay, I'm very current in this field I have chosen to work in.* Being current is very important to me. The other thing I remember thinking was, *Oh my goodness, nothing is new.* I graduated in the 1980s. If I was to step back and say, *In terms of nourishing ourselves and our bodies, what do we really need to know?* nothing has dramatically changed, and yet we still have problems. We have more information than ever before and yet much of the population is in terrible shape. The problem is it is too complicated. If someone can make it simple and compelling and we focus on kids, then we can really impact the future in a positive way. Lightning bolt: *This is my job. This is what I'm going to do.*

I conceived of Rainbow Plate while sitting on a park bench in New York City. I realized the world does not need me to do another lecture on, you know, carbohydrate metabolism. I literally had this image of a rainbow plate; this notion of making it simple for kids. The more colours that are on your plate, the healthier your diet. It's that clear and simple. I shifted gears mentally. It took me a long time to actually have the courage to act on it. I started to talk about it. I started actually doing things that would move me in that direction. I bought the domain name and I registered it. I was still lecturing for several more years. It's funny because I still receive messages and emails from former students who write, "Oh I remember when you talked about the Rainbow Plate and how you were going to do this. Now you are doing it and that's awesome."

I eventually left the teaching job to focus full-time on making this dream happen. What is cool for me is I'm a mom. I've got three kids who are all finding their way in the world, and what has been wonderful for me is being able to show them the vision I had when I was their age. I had the notion of doing this in the world and now all these years later I'm actually doing it. I have come full circle. The hilarious thing is that I once sold candy for a living.

It really has been a journey. The message for me is that all is good. Every part of the journey, even some of it that may seem ridiculous or unrelated, every piece of it contributes to where I am today.

WE ARE SOLD so much on these lightning-bolt moments. People write books and movies about them. What Janet's lightning bolt moment taught me is years of cumulative experience ignites that moment of knowing. We can all long for that one epiphany and fail to notice the small surges that we are creating in our own lives. I now see my life as a series of turning points and lightning bolts. Janet's story encouraged me to look back on my life to notice what was written in my past. What I see there is this overwhelming desire to be supported and recognized for my true nature, for who I am.

Questions for Self-Reflection

1. Nature, vegetables, and fruit inspire Janet. What inspires you? Take a look at your list. How can you invite more of those inspiring things into your life?

2. Janet sat in a lecture theatre and heard a message that really resonated with her. What messages have you heard that spoke to you and made you think, *I would like to do that?* I am sure you have felt it at some point in your life. If you haven't, how could

you shift your perspective so you really take notice when you these messages come?

3. Janet overcame her sense of not fitting in when she came to terms with who she was and was able to say, "This is me." When have you felt, even for just a fleeting moment, "This is me"? What were you doing? Who were you with? Where were you? How did you feel?

4. Where, with whom, and how can you create more of those "This is me" experiences in your life?

5. By creating the Rainbow Food Education Foundation, Janet has created a community that shares her desire to make healthy eating simple. What steps could you take to create a community around you to move your ideas forward?

Creative Solutions to Rethink Community

MARY-KATE GILBERTSON

Passionate Community Builder, Owner of Kaboom
Consulting, Consulting Partner in Two Sisters River,
Associate at Shared Value Solutions and Karen Farbridge
and Associates, and Shareholder in Anwaatin Inc.

We are all here to get up to something and our lives would be different if we focused on that.

I MET MARY-KATE GILBERTSON at an Open Space facilitation course in Guelph, Ontario. We had a mutual friend and we spoke together over lunch. Her energy is contagious. She is fanatical about connection and making her community the best place to live, which is ironic because she didn't start out that way. For eight years Mary-Kate worked on a large multi-million-dollar project in Sudbury, Ontario, for an environmental consulting firm, doubting whether she was the right person for the job. She lived in Guelph but routinely commuted to Sudbury to work on the project. She liked Guelph but wasn't at all engaged in the community. She was angry about her career, pretty committed to maintaining a degree of isolation, and kept people at arm's length. Mary-Kate describes her turning point as a Reiki session she skeptically went to upon the recommendation of a friend. Her intention was clarification about her work. The result was the unleashing of an incredibly active and connected woman.

Mary-Kate is a passionate community builder who seeks to change the paradigm of how we live in urban spaces. She is dedicated to catalyzing resilient, workable, connected, and empowered communities. She has a bachelor of science degree from the University of Plymouth, England, and a master of science degree from the University of Windsor, Ontario. Mary-Kate has more than twenty years of work experience in the environmental field, specializing in climate action, cap and trade readiness, community energy plans, educational outreach, community sustainability planning, community and public consultation, human health and ecological risk assessment, environmental site assessment, and contaminated site remedial action planning.

Mary-Kate has been instrumental in the development of an urban intentional community in her neighbourhood. She has worked with not-for-profits like eMERGE Guelph, the Trillium Waldorf School, Transition Guelph, and the Junction Neighbourhood Group to help them grow and maintain their community visions. She and her partner, Mike, started Two Sisters River, which includes an urban farm and a number of social enterprises such as Backyard Bok Boks, a backyard chicken business that provides everything you need to start raising your own backyard chickens, and The Purple Cow Hostel, which uses the sharing economy and volunteer support to create a hub for travellers. Mary-Kate is committed to making things happen. She is a catalyst for social and environmental change.

Mary-Kate believes in possibilities and is here to "get up to something." She is passionate about moving the world to greater connection and belonging. In creating an intentional community in her neighbourhood, she let go of the traditional view of what a neighbourhood is supposed to be. She learned at a young age that she had the ability to solve problems and direct her energy toward making what she wanted happen, even if it meant moving past cultural norms.

Key messages from Mary-Kate:

- Powerfully stand for your purpose and make decisions to move in that direction.
- Move beyond what culture tells you not to do.
- Push beyond your comfort zone.
- Who you are is the source of your power.
- You are the driver of your own solutions.
- Just do it and do it imperfectly.
- Talk about what is important to you.
- You are capable. Create your own way.

———

I THINK LIFE is about giving ourselves over to a higher purpose and then powerfully standing in this purpose and making decisions that help us to move toward it. It is really locking into our own power as human beings. I think the source of our power is like unlocking who we are as individuals and unabashedly and unapologetically leading passionate and inspired lives.

Our culture tells us not to do this. It tells us to settle down and understand the limitations of the real world. I like really busting through this and then leaning into how we can create our own reality. Whatever we strongly stand for, what we really source from, is already happening. If we lean into our dreams, or our intentions, then it's going to happen for sure.

I think that we are all here to get up to something. I think that our lives would be so different if we were focused on that. If we were able to say, *Okay, this is what I'm here to do.* I am really visioning for the moment and thinking, *How can we create Guelph as a model of the future city? What are all the pieces that would be really amazing in there and what would that look like?* Then I chart my course and if I never make it, I still feel like I've done great things.

I am thinking about my own city in a different way and in my immediate world around me. The thing that really gets my blood pumping is how we create our lives in a different way. Mike and I started out living in a shared house. That was really great—really thinking about community and living with community. Then we just kind of busted out of that model, and now we have kids and we want our friends to live nearby and we want us all to share things. So instead of thinking we had to get over that shared housing idea, we had to get on with our lives, we were, "Yah, let's make it happen." So we just started creating it, an intentional community. What has been interesting is that just by doing it and doing it imperfectly, and not having it all work out, it has just come into being.

What is really exciting is we had just two people on our street who started talking about how we could do things a bit differently, and out of that conversation, this whole community has emerged in a really short space of time. You know, people buy houses close to us now. We have this gang of children who are running around. We close down our road and do a weekly potluck. I am surrounding myself with people who stand for me in the world and I stand for them. We don't talk about the weather much. We're talking at a different level. We are meeting each other in the street or in the car park and we are talking about life straight away. We are talking about what is important to us.

Now it is cool because people are telling *me* about this, you know, asking, "Have you heard about this community?" and it's my community they are talking about. It's neat because people feel like what is happening is something really different. What is happening is how we used to live, how life used to be—connected. It's really not that different. It's just that we envisioned it for right now. For me, the vision is just kind of who I am. I can't help it. It is just kind of bubbling out of me all the time. When I'm on the right track, my life feels amazing. I know I'm on the right track when I have the time and the space to appreciate my life, my children, my husband, and this community, and I'm not running trying to create the next thing. I don't always get the balance right.

I wasn't always engaged in my community. I lived in Guelph and I liked Guelph, but I didn't really know anybody. I went to work and I came home. That was it, and I was pretty committed to just maintaining a degree of isolation. I was outgoing but I kept people at arm's length. I was careful about not letting people get too close to me.

A turning point in my life was a Reiki session. I was really angry then. I didn't really know what I was angry about, but I was holding a lot of anger. I had anger about my work situation. I was pretty skeptical about Reiki, but a good friend had recommended the guy, so I gave it a try. I went to the session wanting clarification about my work situation. At the beginning of the session, I remember the guy rubbing his hands together and saying, "Okay, here we go, the unleashing of Mary-Kate," and it was like this incredibly powerful clearing out. Something unleashed, it was like water. I had a whole bunch of visions of water and of breaking glass. Something was coming apart and reforming. It was an incredibly powerful session. I don't even know what happened but something just changed.

After that session, I went home and I remember almost feeling like I was mourning. I was mourning these people that were—it was like I knew them and they were supposed to be here and they weren't. It was quite a powerful feeling. It felt like someone I knew had died, and I am pretty sure now that it was my family. It was like these people who were supposed to be here and they weren't here. It was one of the first points in my life that I realized, *Oh my gosh, I actually really want to have a family.* That was December, and I went out on a first date with my now-husband on January 15.

It is important to understand how you measure success. Usually we measure success by how much is in our bank account. There are a lot better metrics than that. My metrics are related to how my life feels. It is related to how many incredible people surround me, and what I am part of creating. I like the feeling that I'm up to no good, that I've got things happening, that I'm pushing the boundaries. If nobody is complaining about anything that I'm doing, then I'm probably not doing enough. It's good to have a bit in your bank account too.

I have phenomenal parents. They are amazing. They are very different from each other, but they both were so great at always letting us know that whatever we wanted to do, we could do. I was really into horses when I was growing up. I rode often, so my parents got me a pony when I was eleven or something. At some point they came to me and told me they were not going to be able to keep paying the amount of money that was needed to keep the pony. It was more money than the family could commit to. Here I was eleven and I loved this pony. I was like, "What do you mean?" What was cool about that process was that I started working through some solutions for me to keep the pony. My parents never said to me, "No that won't work, you can't do that." They totally let me work out the solutions for it. They shared the problem that we needed to look at and asked, "What do you think we should do about it?" They allowed me to be the driver of the solutions. This was really empowering for me to get at eleven years old—that if there is something in the way of what I want to do, then I can make it happen.

So the solution was that I rented my room out. Dad and I built this special little bed in what was essentially a storage room. It was like this little box room. It was so small you wouldn't even put a bed in it, so we built this tiny little bed that had this desk underneath it and I rented out my bedroom for the next four years and the money went toward my pony.

———

TO HEAR FROM Mary-Kate that she was once angry and isolated because of her career offered me such reassurance. My experience of Mary-Kate was that she was anything but angry and isolated; she was connected and thriving. I felt that if she could make that shift, it was possible for me to make it as well. It is possible for all of us to make the shift to thriving.

Questions for Self-Reflection

1. What do you need to let go of in order to unabashedly and unapologetically lead an inspired life?

2. Mary-Kate knows she is on the right track when she has the time and the space to appreciate her life, her children, her husband, and her community. How do you know when you are on track?

3. Mary-Kate learned at a young age that she had the ability to solve problems and direct energy toward making what she wanted happen. What skills did you learn at a young age that can help you today?

4. Mary-Kate and her husband made a conscious decision about what type of community they wanted to create around them, and they made it happen. What kind of community would you like to be surrounded by? What is one small step you could take to start to create that community around you?

5. Mary-Kate's metrics for measuring her success aren't about money; they are about how her life feels. What metrics are you using to measure success? How would you like your life to feel?

Learning an Intentional Approach to Life

SANDI STRIDE

Founding President and CEO,
Sustainable Hamilton Burlington

> *There is a spiritual element to how natural succession happens. It is miraculous.*

I FIRST MET SANDI Stride at a sustainability event when I was vice-president of environmental performance. The enthusiasm and vivacity that she brought to her work were in stark contrast to the way I felt about mine. The only thing I really knew about Sandi was that she had moved from London, Ontario, and was starting this sustainability organization from scratch. I got a sense that she had re-created herself a number of times and decided I wanted to know more. I interviewed Sandi at the offices of the organization she founded. It was a beautiful old building that used to be a seed warehouse. The wood floors and brick walls were gorgeous and the light flooded in the amazing windows.

Sandi is the executive director of the Centre for Climate Change Management at Mohawk College and the founding president of Sustainable Hamilton Burlington, a non-profit social enterprise dedicated to helping businesses and organizations thrive by reducing their environmental impact and creating social value. She has a bachelor of science degree in physical geography with a minor in biology from the University of Toronto and a master in business administration degree from Western University's Richard Ivey School of Business.

Sandi is a business strategy, branding, and sustainability expert. Her career has included environmental planning, marketing management with an international packaged goods corporation, advertising, and consulting. Her consulting work has focused on corporate strategy, sustainability strategy, and communications. She is passionate about helping to create sustainable prosperity for the Ontario cities of Hamilton and Burlington.

Sandi's career path is a winding one, and at times a tragic and difficult one that required her to reassess her direction. It is a journey back to a purpose that has lived in her from a young age. She got lost, made decisions from a place of fear, and then really got intentional, and now she is making a difference by bringing businesses and organizations together to advance sustainability.

Key messages from Sandi:

- Pay attention when you feel *There is something that I am meant to do.*
- Look back to your youth—it provides hints to what is important to you.
- Notice when you are making decisions from a place of fear. Those decisions may not be the best for you.
- Trust your instincts.
- Surround yourself with wonderful friends, ones who will support you through dark times.
- There are signs to remind you who you are, when you pay attention.
- Notice what brings you energy and do more of that.
- Become intentional in the way you live your life.
- Doubting yourself is normal. Listen for the messages that confirm you are on the right track.

———————

HOW I WOULD describe myself today is different than how I would have described myself at other points in my life. Now, I feel a lot of fulfillment and joy. I am driven and perhaps more driven than I have ever been. I think it is because I am doing what I was always meant to do. I am doing it because I am called to do it.

Since my teenage years, I have felt there is something I am meant to do. I would never have guessed that this is the form it would take, though. Yet this is what my whole life has been preparing me to do. From an existential point of view, it's an amazing feeling, but it hasn't always been that way.

When I was growing up, I spent a lot of time on Georgian Bay with my family and friends. At twelve years old, my friend and I would pack hotdogs and some matches and venture out in kayaks for a day of exploring. When we were hungry we would stop, cook a couple of hotdogs, and explore some more, then be home for dinner.

That exploring created my very close relationship with nature. By high school I knew I needed to do something related to nature.

I studied physical geography and biology at university. I learned what really makes my heart sing is to look at inter-relationships. Through my ecology courses I learned I am a systems thinker; I enjoyed discovering how things are related. There is a spiritual element to how natural succession happens. It is miraculous.

My first job after university was a water resources technician, then environmental planner, and then I helped the company with marketing. During this time, I came to understand that I really need people. I'm outgoing and I get energy from people. Around that time I was also realizing the importance of getting businesses to understand the impact they have on the environment and to get them onside to do something about it. Then my husband was offered a promotion to move to London, Ontario. To do what I wanted to do, I needed to understand the language of business, so I applied to Western's Ivey School of Business master's program and I was accepted, and graduated. We moved back to Toronto and had two children.

When my kids were six and eighteen months, I got a job as a product manager for one of the world's leading packaged good companies. It was a great experience. I travelled across the country and learned a lot about branding, brand communications, and marketing strategy. The systems thinker in me loved it. I had to understand all aspects of the organization and think at a strategic level. Then my grandparents and father-in-law died within a year and a half of each other, and I was getting a little skeptical about how much difference I was making. We needed a more balanced life. So we moved back to London and my husband went back to school. I got a job at an advertising agency.

I was eventually invited to become partner in the firm, which meant a significant financial investment. The associate creative director of the firm and I looked at the offers and realized we could invest a lot of money for a little part of this business or we could

invest a little money and start our own marketing and communications company. We did that. It was a lot of fun. We had offices in
both London and Toronto.

Then my marriage fell apart. My ex-husband moved back to
Toronto and I was left once more to rethink my life. As the single mom
I had just become, there was too much travelling back and forth to
Toronto. In advertising, I was conflicted about helping companies
sell stuff I didn't believe in. What I wanted was to help businesses
that I really believed in to succeed. I sold my shares in the advertising agency. That was like going through another divorce. I started
a consulting firm to do strategic planning and brand strategy.

Then I ended up in a relationship with someone new. Someone
I thought was just going to be the love of my life. He was highly
educated and just a wonderful, wonderful man. I was feeling really
vulnerable at the time and I missed the signs of his mental health
issues and overlooked his very controlling nature. I had a lot of
fears at the time. Fears of not making enough money, not being
able to support my kids, fear of being a bag lady. Fear was driving
my decisions and we eventually got married.

Shortly after that, he had a breakdown. We really struggled.
His controlling nature challenged my sense of self. I had to shut
down his business, deal with Revenue Canada, and manage to
keep us afloat. Between us we had five children and I was working
to support us all. It was a really difficult environment and my kids
moved back to live with their father. In that really horrible time, I
was losing myself and that forced me to get professional help. The
darkness lasted seven years and ended with his suicide.

My friends got me through. I have a group of the most wonderful women friends and they were my sanity. So when he died,
people came out of the woodwork concerned about me: my former
business partner, family, friends, business associates, all saying,
"This is not your fault!" It still brings tears to my eyes.

After that, there was a lot of introspection on my part. Looking
very deeply inside helped me to understand who I am. I came out

of that the person who I fundamentally am, who I was meant to be. I just got so lost for a few years. I'd really gotten off track. I hadn't been intentional about what I wanted to do. I was jumping at the opportunities that were put in front of me and a lot of it was out of fear.

Just before my husband died, I came across an article written by one of my ecology professors. It was an article about air pollution. It was an "Ah-ha!" moment. How had I gotten so far away from what is important to me? This is who I am. Then I was driving to Toronto, listening to the CBC, and there was a documentary about Interface Carpet's Belleville plant and how the city had come in to check their meters because they felt there must be some sort of malfunction. They had reduced their water consumption by 90 percent by applying sustainability principles. I was already on the path but this solidified it, it just crystalized it for me: this was exactly the direction I needed to be taking.

I got back to going places and doing things I wanted to do. I went to Bali with a friend. There I was introduced to a shaman who owned this incredible spa. I had a treatment with this guy. Before he did anything, he looked at my palm and he said, "Oh, you've had a hard life, but you have paid for bad karma. You have a new beginning now, a new life. Go and enjoy your new life." I couldn't believe it. It gave me chills. That afternoon, afterwards, sitting on the terrace outside my room on the edge of the jungle, I hardly even moved. I just experienced in a way that I never had before. The colours and the sounds of the jungle. I could hear all the sounds— the birds and the gecko, everything with new clarity. I had never experienced this incredible sense of peace; like total, fundamental, deep, deep peace. And I thought, *This truly is a new beginning.*

I became intentional. I did a ten-year plan. I felt that I had leadership potential and wanted to be in a position where I would bring businesses together for the betterment of the environment, the community, and our world overall. I also decided that by the time I was sixty I wanted to have a partner to share my retirement years.

I met this wonderful man online. We have been together ever since. I left London and we bought a house together that was accessible to the Greater Toronto Area for work and surrounded by nature, both important to us.

I started to work in the Hamilton area. The city was in the midst of a transformation. The city's brand image as a polluted, heavy-industrial steel town really was unjustified now. I thought, *I can help to improve the brand of this city through sustainability.* There were some really strong environmental organizations, but nobody was talking to businesses about sustainability and I saw a real need here for that. I decided a non-profit would be more accessible to businesses than a for-profit business, so I started Sustainable Hamilton.

In the early days, it was like rolling water uphill. I felt so exposed doing this all alone and not getting any financial support. I started to question myself: *It is so hard! Is this really what I am supposed to do? Is it supposed to be so hard? How much more of myself do I put into this before I step back and try something else? Is it really the right thing to do?*

My now-husband, a coach, my wonderful women friends— and several new ones—once again helped keep me on track, and I forged ahead. Sustainable Hamilton Burlington recently joined a larger network and received some significant funding. We have staff and a new level of credibility. Five and a half years later and I now feel more connected in this community than in the twenty years I lived in London. I know more people, and I feel more sup- ported. Part of it is this accepting community; part of it is I am myself. I'm my authentic self. I guess people are responding to that and the passion I have for this work because it is the right thing to do.

I SEE SANDI'S story as one of reclaiming her true nature, her true purpose in life. Our lives meander and sometimes we get off track, into situations and relationships that cause us to lose connection with who we are and what is important to us. In a sense, writing this book has been about reclaiming myself. It is possible to reclaim ourselves at any age and from any circumstances. All we have to do is just take that first step.

Questions for Self-Reflection

1. Sandi feels more driven now than ever because she is doing what she was always meant to do. That has left her feeling a lot of fulfillment and joy. What brings you fulfillment and joy?

2. The time Sandi spent kayaking Georgian Bay instilled a deep connection to the environment. What were you passionate about in your youth?

3. Sandi understood that she needed people. They gave her energy. So she designed her career and life with that knowledge. What gives you energy? Make a list.

4. From her studies of ecology, Sandi realized her love of seeing the big picture and looking for interconnections. That understanding drove her career decisions. What do you love to do? Where could you apply that passion?

5. If you got intentional about your life, what would your goals be? What would your ten-year plan include?

Happiness and Synchronicity

CHRIS HARTMANN

Potter and Rower

> 66 *I'm just being pushed in the direction I have to go.* 99

I MET CHRIS HARTMANN while walking back home after having a coffee with a friend of mine. It was during the weeklong Henley Rowing Regatta and I was drawn to a sidewalk pottery sale. I felt compelled to cross the road and find out what it was all about. As I was picking up a piece of pottery that intrigued me, Chris arrived by my side and started talking about pottery with exuberance. Something she said caught my attention and I knew I had to interview her. Her words were, "I am the happiest person I know," and she said it with a smile that lit up her face. A week later I was at Chris's home interviewing her.

Chris is founder, teacher, potter, and creator of A Third Space Pottery Studio. She was in finance until she was laid off and one of her friends suggested she should open a pottery studio and start teaching. That is precisely what she did. For more than twenty years Chris has been honing her skills at various studios throughout the Greater Toronto Area. The name of her studio was inspired by the work of sociologist Ray Oldenburg and refers to a place where people like to hang out. The first space is home, the second space is work, and the third space is where people meet to unwind. A third space could be a café, a bookstore, a park, or a pottery studio.

Her home is a cute cottage with an overgrown garden, an inviting front porch, and the most amazing walnut tree in her backyard. Her basement is her pottery studio, and it is filled with raw clay, partially finished pieces, and the tools of the trade. We sat in her bright, cozy living room that was full of books, cushions, and colour. On her business card, Chris declares, *I am not a minimalist*. I totally understood what that meant when I saw how filled her home was with all that she loved. As we spoke, the sun streamed in the windows.

I must admit I left Chris's home studio feeling a little jealous of just how happy she was. What drove her happiness was that she was doing what she loved. To me, she is such an amazing example of someone who is thriving.

Key messages from Chris:

- When you are doing what you love, make a decision to love all aspects of it—even cleaning the kiln.

- Ask for help. People love helping.
- You don't have to do it all yourself. If there is something you don't like doing and it takes up too much of your time, find someone else to do it who loves that work.
- When you are starting on a goal and feeling like you don't know what you are doing, go and ask the people who are already doing it.
- Choose the freaking mountain that you love and love climbing that mountain
- We are being shaped by the life events that we think are so terrible and so hard. Those events also help us to understand that some things don't matter.

―――――――

I AM THE happiest person I know. It's because I get to do what I love doing and I have control over my destiny. I wake up some mornings before my alarm because I can't wait to go into my studio. I decided to love every aspect of being a potter. People see someone throw a pot in a video online and it looks so quick and easy, but it takes time. Potting is physically tons of work. I just can't resent anything I do as a potter. I have to scrape kiln shelves, rewire the kiln, and put new elements in it. I don't like doing it, but I also just keep thinking that this is all part and parcel of this freakishly happy life that I have. I am not financially successful right now, but I get to figure out how to make that happen and that makes me happy too.

Happiness comes from doing what you love and a little bit of struggle—I love my struggle now. I understand that I have had enough struggle to get to where I want to be. Sometimes a really crappy struggle that didn't seem to be leading anywhere, like a bad divorce, bad jobs, getting laid off, clinical depression, you name it.

The divorce forced me to do things for myself. It's nice to do things as a team and have someone else take some of the responsibility, but there is something very freeing about making all the decisions yourself, not always fun but freeing. The depression made me much more kind-hearted toward people.

In my early fifties I got laid off from my job, which was a good thing. About that same time I came home and my neighbour had put up a For Sale sign. When I asked, "What's going on?" he told me, "We're fed up. We're moving back to Niagara Falls." I was so deeply jealous, I realized I had to make a change. I didn't want to be in Oakville, I wanted to be home, and for me that's Niagara Region.

I was talking with my friend Becky and telling her I can buy a house in Niagara, not have a mortgage, and do something like work at McDonald's or Tim Hortons just to pay my bills. Becky said to me, "Start a pottery studio. Teach." Magic words. I didn't even have to mull it over. I understood. Once I made the decision to move, little by little everything just kept happening the right way.

I found this house and it is exactly the house I wanted. I found it the first day, and my real estate agent, whom I adore, who was doing everything she could not to influence me, just grabbed my knee. We were in the car and she said, "Okay, if this house looks half as good inside as it does on the outside, *I* would want to buy it." She was so excited for me: "Oh look, there is a back entrance, oh and then you have privacy, and oh there is a washroom here, oh the ceiling is high enough."

So I found the perfect house, with the perfect setup to have a little studio. I got the house at a very good price because it was a rental and the renters were drug dealers. You know, those lovely people insulated the garage. I guess they were going to turn it into a grow-op. People were leery of the house so I was able to buy it. I got this great house. I got this great yard. The house is perfect for my studio. I have great neighbours. The location is perfect for me to get around.

I moved in, took a little time to get organized, then called Niagara College: "I hear you give free business advice. I want to start a business." Luckily, I spoke to a woman who said, "Oh, I think we have a program for you."

It was a two-week program for unemployed adults who want to start their own business. I got in. I would get up at 2 a.m. and start writing down the ideas in my head. I had this idea that I would have two potting wheels downstairs, teach one or two people at night, and work at Tim Hortons. The best thing about the class was being with six other people who were also starting a business. They helped me gel my ideas. After I crunched the numbers, I realized with eight wheels I could teach full-time. The more I worked toward the goal of a pottery studio, the more it worked out for me.

I started looking online for second-hand wheels. They're hard to find. I only found one. Then when buying stock at Pottery Supply House, I asked, "Do you know anybody who is selling second-hand wheels?" To my surprise, he responded, "We have some here." As it turns out, they never have second-hand wheels for sale, ever. I just walked in at the right time and bought these wonderful wheels from them.

I knew how to use a kiln, but I didn't know how to take care of a kiln. Low and behold, Pottery Supply House was going to have a course in September on how to maintain a kiln, all the things I had to know. I took the course. Turns out they had never offered a course like that before. It came literally exactly when I needed it.

In my business class was a guy, Glenn, who wanted to start his own bookkeeping business. I was his first client. Even though I worked in finance, I am the worst with money. Glenn just gives me very, very good advice and takes over the part of the job I would hate. If I did it myself, everything would be disorganized; I would be stressed and losing sleep. What would take me forever to do, Glenn does in a couple hours, and I get to use that time in my studio. I finally realized I don't have to do everything myself.

Most potters are generous, very kind, and extremely giving people. They are willing to give you their secrets, willing to take time to help out. I am happy to be part of that world. There are other potters here in town. When I was starting out, I got in my car, drove over to these potters, and introduced myself: "Hi, I'm starting a studio." I thought I might as well do this because I didn't really know what I was doing. Every one of them welcomed me, encouraged me, and gave me great advice. None of them want to teach, so they sent students to me. Each one wished me well. It was lovely, and made me even more sure I was on the right track.

So I started this little studio and have been doing it now for two and a half years. I've had truly the most amazing people come and do pottery with me. I have to make money, so I charge them. It costs money to run the studio, but I want to laugh because honestly the people are so wonderful. They come here. They actually give me money and I get to have them in my house and in my studio. Some of them have decided to become potters. I am glad I got to be the first place they tried potting.

I have learned to ask for help. I used to always think that it was somehow weak to ask for help and I had to do it alone. Now, I take the help. I had bought out three separate potters in the past two years and had carloads of stuff jammed in my garage. One of the guys from my studio helped me organize. We spent eight hours throwing out broken pottery and crappy pottery I'd held on to and pottery that I was holding for people who never came back. Another potter friend walked up the driveway to spend time in the studio, saw us working, and just started helping. Without their help I'd still be dithering on whether or not to toss out useless stuff. Now my stuff is all organized. I have everything listed in an Excel spreadsheet. *It's in the black desk. It's in the orange cabinet.*

A couple of years ago I wouldn't have felt right taking help from people. You know, I think women do that. We feel like we have to do it all by ourselves. It's really not that big a deal. People want to help. I love helping other people. It is really arrogant for someone who doesn't mind helping other people to then say, "I don't want help or I don't need help." It's stupid.

Now, I want to change the way I earn my living. I want to sell more pottery rather than only doing classes, and it's a big risk. I am not doing it for the sake of risk. I am doing it because I really like making pots. I've always loved potting but I was too insecure about selling my work. So, I taught to make a living doing what I love. I plan to teach a little less so I have more time in the studio just potting. I really don't enjoy selling at craft fairs. I don't even like shopping that much but I love shopping online. To align with "do what you love," I would like to sell online and since I'm terrible at Internet stuff I've asked for help with that.

At the end of the day, all the events in my life that I thought were so terrible and so hard helped shape me, helped make me more confident, and helped make me understand that some things don't matter.

So this is my explanation of what I am doing. I am at the bottom of a mountain that I have to climb. I made the decision to climb this particular mountain and I love freaking climbing this mountain. It's not always easy. I've made huge mistakes, huge mistakes! I get over them and I keep going. People keep coming my way to help me out, to show me, to answer questions.

———

WHAT I LEARNED from Chris is the aliveness that comes when you love climbing the freaking mountain you have chosen to climb. Her happiness doesn't just come from potting. It comes from deciding to love every aspect of potting. To me, Chris's story seems to be the ABCs of moving toward a goal. If I were to summarize it, I would say: commit to making it happen, start taking steps toward that goal, tell people what you need to make it happen, ask for help along the way, and receive the help you're offered.

Questions for Self-Reflection

1. Chris fully committed herself to her pottery business. She sold her house with the intention of buying a home in Niagara where she could start her pottery business. Once she made that commitment, things started to happen for her. What have you not fully committed to in your life?

2. Your commitment doesn't have to be as drastic as selling your house and moving to a new city. It could be a commitment to take a class, investigate an opportunity, or update your résumé. What could you commit to that might move you a step toward where you want to go?

3. It is hard not to notice the synchronicity in Chris's pursuit of pottery. Where have you noticed synchronicity show up in your life? What direction does that synchronicity seem to be pushing you?

4. Chris didn't only learn to ask for help, she learned to receive help. Where in your life are you declining the help that is being offered? Practise receiving that help. Notice when you refuse help. When you do refuse help, take a moment to reflect on why. What is at the source of you refusing help?

5. Chris describes the potters as generous, kind, extremely giving, and willing to share their secrets and to help out. Where in your life could you be kinder, more generous, and more willing to help out?

3

STEPPING OUT OF THE DOWNWARD VORTEX

> *The whole world seems to be hostile to dreaming. Hostile and at the same time very hungry and very much in need of a different dream.*

EVELYN ENCALADA GREZ

WHEN I LEFT my job, I did not take the time I needed to truly grieve the loss I felt. I didn't take time to just feel what I was feeling: exhausted, disappointed, angry, and confused. I went right back into "doing mode." Doing is what I know. When I am doing, I feel valued. I wrote. I took courses. I exercised. I got busy thinking about what I wanted to do next. People would tell me to just follow my passion. I wondered how it was possible to follow my passion when at that moment I was stuck in despair. I kept trying. Never sitting with, as Yasmine described, all that is and acknowledging it. It took me some time to delve deeper into the wisdom of all the amazing women who had said yes when I asked them if I could interview them for this book. I was definitely in the downward vortex that Laura Kooji described, but it took me months to actually dive into what it was all about. As I've mentioned, it is impossible to enter the upward spiral until we step out of the downward vortex. When we try to do something from that vortex, it will be misaligned with who we are—our true nature.

What Is the Downward Vortex?

When I finally did investigate that downward vortex, I gained such insight into how I kept myself stuck. The vortex is a mindset. It is the mindset of survival, of scarcity. I hold such gratitude for Laura for having provided the key to understanding what caused me to implode and burn out. I discovered that it was a trap that we can all fall into in our relationships with others and with ourselves. As I read more, I recognized myself in what I read. I saw how it played out in my mind, in my family, in my workplace, and even on the world stage. I realized the trap I had created for myself.

The model of this downward vortex was first developed by Dr. Steven Karpman and is known as the Karpman Drama Triangle. The drama triangle is a model of human strategies for managing fear and anxiety. Playing in the triangle results in being drained of energy and gets in the way of us reaching our greatness or helping others reach theirs.

I explain the vortex a bit differently than Laura. The vortex plays out in almost every fairy tale we have ever read. I like to use *Cinderella* to explain the roles within the vortex because it is a story we all know and there is something about Cinderella that I relate to. There are three roles: the oppressor, the rescuer, and the victim. In *Cinderella*, the oppressor is the Wicked Step-mother, the victim is Cinderella, and the rescuer is the Fairy Godmother. Here is how I would describe the roles of the vortex using the characters from *Cinderella*:

The Wicked Stepmother
Oppressor

The Stepmother is critical, bossy, and domineering. She believes she is right and that there is nothing right about Cinderella. She therefore tells Cinderella what to do and how to do it.

Cinderella
Victim

Her Stepmother thwarts her dream of going to the ball and Cinderella feels powerless to change it.

The Fairy Godmother
Rescuer

The really nice Fairy Godmother swoops in and rescues Cinderella by magically creating an opportunity for Cinderella to go to the ball.

What powers the downward vortex is fear: fear of not being or having enough; fear of losing control; fear of change; fear of not surviving. We each have imprinted in us the brain of the cavewoman who is constantly on alert for changes in her environment so she can react to what threatens her in order to survive. The problem is that we react to psychological threats in the same way we react to the physical threat of the sabre-tooth tiger.

We also have imprinted on our brain every experience we have ever had, and those traumatic moments of hurt, shame, and embarrassment stick with us. They come out to play with us when we least expect it and affect how we react. Understanding those moments and how they trigger us in the here and now helps us to step out of the triangle.

My Dance in the Vortex

Spending time in the vortex left me drained of energy, feeling broken and separate, and those feelings lingered even after I left my job.

So let me tell you about my dance in the vortex. It is not something I am proud of, and I can imagine how different things could have been if I had awareness of this dance before. Yet I know I have learned about it at the perfect time for me. I do find some solace in knowing I did not dance alone. I'm sad to think of how many people danced with me. I have such a feeling of gratitude for finally seeing what I was doing to myself. Now I imagine what the world would be like if we each woke up to our dance and stepped out of the downward vortex.

Me as rescuer

My favourite place to be in the triangle is rescuer. I feel valued when I help people, especially people I see as the underdog.

Helping others makes me feel I am making a difference. As soon as I step into the triangle as a rescuer, I am identifying a victim or victims who need rescuing and an oppressor(s) from whom the victim needs rescuing. As a rescuer, I am aligning myself with the victim, and that victim needs me to save them from that oppressor.

I would not call myself a Fairy Godmother, though. When I am in rescuer mode, I would consider myself more of a super-hero. I can feel that superhero in my body. My shoulders go back, my hands go on my hips, and I can feel my hair and cape blowing in the wind. I can almost hear theme music, something like the *Indiana Jones* theme accompanying me, as I swoop in and rescue people. I rescue people before they know they need rescuing. I even rescue people who don't want to be rescued. I rescue situations too, putting out fires before they start. All this makes me feel valued and purposeful, until it doesn't. What I am crying out for when I am rescuing is to be noticed and appreciated for all that I'm doing. It would also be amazing if someone would remind me that I don't have to rescue everyone or every situation. What I need when I am in rescue mode is for someone to tell me to slow down and set some boundaries, and nurture myself so I don't exhaust myself.

With all that running around saving people, I become absolutely exhausted. I start to wonder why nobody has noticed all my rescuing and, more to the point, why aren't they helping me with that rescuing? Ultimately, it is the oppressor of all those victims I have been rescuing that I believe should be doing something about it. I then get frustrated and angry that I am not getting any support in doing all this work.

Me as oppressor

As soon as I start getting angry, I move into the oppressor position in the triangle. I begin to victimize the people whom

I perceived were oppressing the people I was rescuing. This is when I start fighting what is—fighting with the metaphorical hose from the yoga centre. I become the person who knows best. I start telling people what to do. I get critical, bossy, and domineering. I can feel that fight in my body as well, and it does not feel good at all. I am tense from head to toe, and I point the finger of one hand and my other hand is resting stiffly on my hip. Not surprisingly, I meet resistance from the people I am oppressing. I feel like they don't listen to me. They don't understand me. I get more frustrated and angry. Then I start to really not like myself.

What I yearn for most when I find myself the oppressor is for someone to stand with me. I long for someone to meet me with compassion and say, "You're angry. I get that. You have every right to be angry. Tell me about what's going on for you." Anger is an interesting emotion. We all experience it, and yet we all have been programmed to not like it, to resist that feeling in ourselves and to turn our backs on it when someone else is expressing it. That is where Laüra Hollick's words of being an ecosystem are so helpful. Rather than seeing anger as an obstacle, I am learning to welcome it into my ecosystem and start to explore it.

When I actually spent time just being, I sat with what I was feeling and followed Yamsine's advice to just sit with all that is. I withheld judgment, not making anything or anybody wrong or right, just acknowledging that it was there. I allowed myself to just be for a while. What opened up for me was an awareness of what I longed for in life—to be supported and to be recognized and appreciated for who I am. Interestingly enough, I discovered that I was looking for support, recognition, and appreciation from the wrong people. I also had the epiphany that I may have been the biggest offender by not appreciating and supporting myself.

Me as victim

I start to really not like myself and I beat myself up for my behaviour and my seeming ineffectiveness. I slide into the victim role. As a victim, I feel helpless, powerless, like I have worked so hard and there is absolutely nothing more I can do to change anything. I withdraw. What I feel in my body here is like I am melting. I call me as victim "Melting Cinderella," a cross between Cinderella and the Oz's Wicked Witch of the West after the water has been thrown on her. Instead of crying out, "I'm melting. I'm melting," my cry of despair is, "Help me. Help me."

When I am Melting Cinderella, what I long for is someone to wrap their arms around me (literally or figuratively) and tell me, "It's okay. You will be okay. You need time to rest. You have worked so hard and you just need to take some time and look after yourself for a while. You are so capable. You have accomplished so much. Take some time for yourself and you will get your energy back again. I am here for you when you are ready to start again." Truth be told, those are the words I most need to hear from myself. As Paddy Torsney taught, words of self-compassion are so powerful for moving forward.

When I look at myself in the vortex, I see myself as engaging the chaos around me and within me. When I step out of the chaos and ground myself in who I am, my true nature, it is possible to disengage from the chaos and become a compassionate witness to it.

Know Your Own Dance

Have you seen yourself playing any of those roles: victim, oppressor, rescuer? Awareness is the first step in any shift. Knowing how you dance in the vortex and who your favourite partners are makes stepping out of the vortex that much easier. *Here are some steps to take to prepare you to leave the triangle behind for good.*

1. **Be aware of when you are dancing in the triangle.**

2. **Notice where you are in the triangle.**
   - What is your preferred role?
   - What does your body feel like when you are in that role?
   - What would you name the character you most like to play in the triangle?
   - If you play one role in the triangle, you play them all. Sleuth out what the other triangle characters feel like in your body.

3. **Pay attention to what situations or relationships trigger you to play the different roles of the triangle.**

4. **Ask yourself tough questions about what keeps you in the triangle.**
   - What are you getting from playing the different characters? (Attention? Power? Acceptance? Empathy? A sense of feeling valued? Needed? An excuse not to follow your dreams?)
   - What are you most looking for when you fall into the roles? (To be heard? Appreciated? Understood? Supported? Have your emotions or you validated?)

5. **Next time you are facing a situation or relationship that triggers you, choose just to sit and notice what is going on for you.**
   - Just breathe through it and get curious about yourself, the situation, and the roles of others in the room.
   - What do you hear yourself saying?

6. **Take the actions to avoid the vortex and step out of the triangle.** In Appendix 4, you will find a Vortex Dance Worksheet to guide you to a greater awareness of yourself in the downward vortex. If you would like some ideas about how to end your dance in the vortex, check out my website: www.AlisonBraithwaite.com/In-Her-Own-Words.

The Downward Vortex as an Ecosystem

If I were going to describe the downward vortex as an ecosystem, it would be the deep ocean, where the sun doesn't shine and strange organisms lurk unseen. I think of the upward spiral as a tropical rainforest, full of life and diversity. These two opposing forces—the upward spiral of being and becoming and the downward vortex of the drama triangle—provide a graphic representation of how to move into a thriving life. The move involves consciously stepping out of a triangular world into a cyclical world. It is a shift from surviving to thriving, and it starts in the minds of each of us.

The best way out of the triangle is to be your own Fairy Godmother, be your own best friend. Really listen to what you are longing for and give that to yourself.

So we may have a map to step out of the vortex created by the drama of the human interactions around us, but how do we enter the upward spiral?

4

EMBRACING THE UPWARD SPIRAL

———

66 *Instead of* who am I, *it's* who can I be? 99

JOCELYN MERCER

NTERING THE SPIRAL into thriving requires a shift in mindset. In essence, the upward spiral that Laüra Hollick described is like travelling around a circle. A circle has no beginning and no end. A circle creates a natural container in which everything is interconnected. A circle is whole. As we move around the circle, we come back to the same place over and over again. If we allow it, with each pass around the circle something is transformed. Those passages around the circle are the upward spiral.

Thriving is about stepping out of a way of thinking (denying parts of ourselves) and into a new way of being (expressing our true nature), and for some it can be a difficult transition. For others, it can take just a moment to wake up to their true nature. Each of the women's stories is a beautiful example of the shift from the fear of the survival mind into the courage of the thriving mind. When I say courage, it is not necessarily the courage to go out and slay dragons. It may start with the courage to be vulnerable, to feel what you are feeling and move through it. It is the courage to ask for the support you need from the people who are best able to provide it. Jennifer Garbin and Jocelyn Mercer would both agree that the opposite of fear is love. They would describe the shift in mindset to enter the upward spiral as a shift from fear to love. There is something about the word *love* that just relaxes me into myself and that seems to be a beautiful place to start anything from. Love is the place to begin thriving from. Perhaps the courage we need is just to be love even when we may not feel that loving in the moment.

The women's stories are about shifts in awareness, perspectives, and emotions, all of which help to create a thriving life. It is about stepping out of seeing ourselves as wounded or broken, and stepping into seeing ourselves as whole. When we regard ourselves as broken or wounded, we approach life from a place of fear. When we understand ourselves to be whole, we are able to courageously create a thriving life that grows from the full expression of our true nature in each moment.

What I learned from these women is that we all struggle. We have all experienced moments of feeling isolated, hurt, alone, different, or not good enough. We all have thoughts and beliefs that limit our growth, our ability to become the person we have always dreamed of being. The pressures of who and what we are supposed to be can bury the truth of who we actually are. Learning the difference between something that calls us from within and something that feels imposed externally is important for stepping into our own possibilities. Finding the intersection between what we are passionate about and what the world needs from us can provide our sense of purpose, our North Star, and our guiding light to navigate our life. We figure out what that is by trying things out and learning what lights us up. Unearthing who we are, connecting to our "being," unleashes the power that drives us to manifest what we have been called to achieve. Having that sense of purpose keeps us from getting lost in the doing of life—all that busyness that can get in the way of just being.

Our thoughts and beliefs about ourselves and others can prevent us from realizing our full potential. When I feel stuck or entangled, I like to take the time to let go and be. Life is not a race to the finish line; it is a poem or a flower unfolding. In order to flow through what Laüra Hollick described as a constant spiral of being and becoming—of creating and re-creating ourselves—I have learned that I need to step out of the beliefs and judgments that hold me in place and step into the energy of who I am becoming.

By interviewing this collection of women, I discerned from them five steps that we can consciously take to enter the upward spiral of being and becoming. The five steps may not happen in sequence. They may happen simultaneously or in tandem. They could take years to manifest or they could happen in an instant. As we travel around the upward spiral, we come back to the same points. As we grow, we see them from a different perspective. As we spiral upward, there is an opportunity to get more clear about who we are, to more deeply let go of what holds us back, find new ways to nurture ourselves, and grow beyond the limitations our minds have set for us.

Step 1. Be Nature

> 66 *Whoever created you did not make a mistake.* 99
> NICKOLETTE REID

See yourself as an ecosystem: many parts that ultimately want to work together. When you view yourself this way, you are whole, resilient, creative, and interconnected, and you embrace the cycles of your life.

When something presents itself as an obstacle, Laüra Hollick welcomes it into her ecosystem. An ecosystem accepts that it is an interconnected community of the living and physical environment, each working together to create a healthy whole. When we perceive ourselves this way, we stop labelling aspects of ourselves as right or wrong, good or bad, too this or too that, not enough this or not enough that. When we drop the labelling, we drop the judgment of ourselves and free up energy to move forward with who we are and welcome the cycles of our life.

Accept back your exiled parts

What came to mind for me when I heard Laüra's description was the story of the reintroduction of wolves into Yellowstone National Park. The early settlers feared the wolf, feeling wolves got in the way of their survival. Labelling them as "bad," they eliminated all the wolves from the continental United States. When the wolves were reintroduced into Yellowstone, the ecosystem within the park started to thrive. Species that had not been seen in the park for years came back. The health and diversity of the park's ecosystem grew exponentially. If you would like to see how welcoming the wolves back into Yellowstone caused it to thrive, watch *How Wolves Change Rivers*, a short video by Sustainable Human.

The elimination of the wolves is such a beautiful metaphor for what we do to ourselves. We have a tendency to exile parts of ourselves that we label as "not good enough," "not strong enough," "too strong," "not intelligent enough," "too intelligent," "too big," "too small," "not quite right," "not like everyone else." You name it, we judge it, and in our judgment we fight against ourselves. Often we expend energy fighting against ourselves: arguing with ourselves about what food we should eat, how we should look, what we should do, what we didn't do, or how we behaved. That fight creates a conflict within ourselves and that takes energy. When we are able to drop the internal struggle, so much is freed up. The energy that we use to keep parts of ourselves hidden or exiled is energy we could be using to thrive. Ultimately this view is about, to use Mary-Kate Gilbertson's words, radical self-acceptance—when we accept ourselves fully, the fight within us ends.

We can start to look at what it means to thrive, a definition that will be unique to each of us, just as it is unique to each of the ecosystems we find on earth. Create the ecosystem you are meant to be, not the one everyone else is telling you that you should be.

You as a thriving ecosystem

The wolves held a key to the thriving of an ecosystem. Like the wolves, the parts of ourselves that we have exiled or made wrong or incomplete may be the key to who we are, our nature—the key to our ability to thrive. It may be time to stop fighting yourself and accept all of you just as you are. Remember that Gloria Roheim McRae turned everything that made her different into an asset, a strength—she turned her differentiator into a gift. You can do that too.

We each have a unique definition of thriving and that definition may evolve over time. It is worth coming back to review and revise what thriving means to you. So many aspects, so many parts ultimately have to work together to create ourselves as a thriving ecosystem. When we focus on only some parts, others may get neglected, which will affect our ability to thrive. When I consider the parts of my thriving ecosystem, what I come up with is:

- physical health
- mental health
- emotional health
- spiritual connection (connection to something bigger than yourself)
- relationships and community
- career
- financial health
- space (the physical environment around you, your home)

Taking the time to contemplate and get really clear about what thriving looks like for you will facilitate the creation of your thriving life.

Step 2. Root into Your Nature

66 *The source of our power is unlocking who we are as an individual and unabashedly and unapologetically leading passionate and inspired lives.* 99

MARY-KATE GILBERTSON

Knowing who you are and what drives you forward helps you to root into your nature. We can be so influenced by others, the media, the culture in which we live that we can find ourselves separated from who we really are. We can feel misaligned when we are living or working within a system or a framework that leaves us feeling like we don't belong. It is difficult to spiral into our next becoming without a solid understanding of who we are.

Rooting into your nature is about discovering your nature, connecting with your calling, understanding your guiding principles, and using your big dream for the world as your guiding light through life. This is where you get in touch with what really matters to you. The women in this book provided a wealth of richness for discovering your nature and rooting into it.

Your true nature

No matter what you think, you have felt your true nature. Our true nature is most apparent when we are feeling most alive, energized, and fully ourselves. Those moments come when we are doing what we love, experiencing what we love, and so totally in the present moment that nothing else matters. Our true nature blossoms when we live beyond the limits of what we thought possible for ourselves.

The world needs you as your most alive, energized, and amazing self. It is from that place of aliveness that you make your best decisions for your work, your life, your community, and the world.

I invite you to spend a moment every morning evoking that sense of who you are, of being fully alive, energized, and yourself. Start your day from a place of being your amazing self and see what opens up for you.

Intersection

Evelyn Encalada Grez invites us to dream as custodians of the planet. Jennifer Garbin believes we are called to the place where our "deep gladness and the world's deep hunger meet." When we look at the stories of these women, we can see how they apply these principles. Janet Nezon's passion for nutrition, and the beauty and colour of fruits and vegetables, collided with the problem of our society's unhealthy eating habits to create her Rainbow Plate. Devon Fiddler's calling was where her love for fashion met the world's hunger for empowering Indigenous women. Understanding what brings you joy and knowing what really matters to you allows you to live with intention and purpose. Sandi Stride saw the need for applying the language of business to manifest a more sustainable world. I invite you to reflect on what that intersection may be for you.

You may immediately understand where the intersection of your gladness and the world's hunger lies, or you may have no clue at all. That's just fine; it gives you an opportunity to put Jody Steinhauer and Chris Hartmann's advice to work—ask for help and look for role models. It's time to have those conversations that matter. Start talking to people about what you have discovered about your deepest gladness and the world's deep hunger that seems to call you. Talk to your family, your friends, your neighbours. Talk to the stranger sitting alone on the park bench or beside you on the bus. Talk to the chief executive officer that you meet at a conference. Talk to anyone that you feel called to engage with. Wisdom can flow from some of the most unusual sources. Remember to be open to receiving the help that is offered.

Tell the people around you what you discovered about yourself and ask them what they might know that could guide you and move you forward. They may suggest a book to read, a person to talk with, an organization that might interest you. When it resonates with you, follow their simple instructions—you may be surprised where it leads. I have found that I am always amazed about what I learn when I sit down with someone and talk about things that really matter. Start the conversations with the intention that you will get clarity about where your gladness and the world's hunger intersect.

What you naturally do

It was natural for Nickolette Reid to know what looked good on people, and she created a business doing that. Yasmine Kandil was naturally creating theatre with young garbage pickers in the slums of Cairo before she even knew what applied theatre was.

Understanding what you naturally do can provide insights into your purpose.

Reading your turning points

Sometimes we neglect to look back on our life to see the turning points that brought us to where we are. When we look back at where we came from, it is easier to see the way forward. Turning points are those moments that offer us a precious gift—whether we have labelled them as good or bad, they are part of our experience and can help us to understand our purpose. When I interviewed Janet Nezon, she could clearly see how everything she had done prepared her for the work she was meant to do. There was even a moment in university with the guest lecturer when she said to herself, *I want to do what she is doing.* Sandi Stride's story is similar. She had a clear understanding of what she wanted to do when she was young. She then went out and collected what she needed to know to do just that.

One of Evelyn Encalada Grez's turning points in life happened before she was born. A military coup in Chile was a key driver in her dream for the world—a world without borders. Evelyn's life predestined her for working as an activist for the rights of temporary farm workers. Gloria Roheim McRae says her childhood predestined her to see things from a different angle. Christine Dernederlanden's life predestined her to help people through their grief. We can learn so much about ourselves when we get curious about our turning points.

Exploring your childhood values and principles

Laura Kooji and Yasmine Kandil both guided their lives based on the values their culture instilled in them. For Laura, the Seven Grandfather Teachings provided her with the values of bravery, honesty, humility, love, respect, truth, and wisdom. The Thirteen Grandmother Moon Teachings guided her to live in harmony with the cycles of the earth and as a woman to honour the connection she has to the cycles of the moon. For Yasmine, it was the values of her Muslim upbringing. She was taught to live life in moderation, with dignity, to support others, and to speak up for those who are not able to speak up for themselves. She was taught to live each day like it is a gift. Both women relied on their cultural teachings to help them through tough times.

Jocelyn Mercer chose love as her premise for life. She aligns herself with love and makes clear decisions based on love. Jody Steinhauer has built her brand on values. If anything gets in the way or potentially clouds her beliefs, her brand, or who she is, then she knows that is the wrong decision to make, the wrong path to go down. Understanding your values will support you in life. It is easier to make decisions when you know they are aligned with who you are and what you believe in.

Our values tend to drive us forward. When the environment we find ourselves in does not align with our values, it can trigger us into anger and frustration. Knowing your values creates awareness. Being able to clearly express them can facilitate dialogue about situations that don't align with who you are.

Step 3. Make Mulch

> 66 *Sometimes you have to let some things go to achieve what you want to be.* 99
> DEVON FIDDLER

Invariably as we spiral up into our next becoming, we will come face to face with limits and beliefs that have served us in the past but will only hold us back as we move into our next becoming. Lisa Belanger learned to live beyond the limiting beliefs her New Brunswick neighbourhood had instilled in her. Jane Hanlon got over her quivering knees and occasional foot-in-mouth incidents for the sake of creating climate resilience. Gloria Roheim

McRae got busy breaking down the boxes that tried to contain her as she lived into the full expression of herself. Jennifer Garbin's perspective about the role of women and members of the LGBTQ community in the church transformed as she created and re-created herself.

Spiralling upwards with ease means letting go of what no longer serves you. To let go, first become aware of how you limit yourself. Begin to question your beliefs and judgments, shift your perspectives about your past, and rewrite your stories.

We carry so many stories and beliefs about ourselves and the world around us that are disempowering. Making mulch of those stories and beliefs is about transforming them from the disempowering to the empowering, or at least to a neutral place. The transformation happens when we are able to shift our mindsets. It's not about forcing yourself to think happy thoughts or repeating positive affirmations in an attempt to be better, it is about really looking at the thoughts and beliefs that may limit you. Imagine how we could transform if we were able to harvest the power and wisdom of the stories of our life experiences.

Let go of supposed-to's

Lisa Belanger spoke about the fences, limitations, or supposed-to's that she was raised with. She spoke about the need to break free of those supposed-to's to make the difference she was called to make in the world: change the health-care system. After university, Gloria Roheim McRae bought into the North American dream: get an education, a job, and a good partner and buy a home, and she did just that. The result was total misalignment and a period of depression. Once she broke out of the box that her supposed-to's put her in, she was able to create the life that aligned with who she truly was.

Understanding the supposed-to's with which we have been raised and assessing whether they still truly serve who we are and who we want to become is an important step in creating that upward spiral in life. Just being aware of your supposed-to's begins the process of letting go. With an awareness, there is an opportunity to choose something different.

Shift perspectives

Sheena Repath was able to shift her perspective of herself as a terrible student when her teacher said to her, "You just process things differently." Nickolette Reid shifted her perspectives about the stories or beliefs she had held about other people. Those beliefs caused her to feel anger, hatred, and disgust. She let go of the stories and was able to write "I forgive you" letters. Rather than thinking from her own perspective, she shifted to the perspective of the other people involved and how they had grown up. With that shift came understanding. Her anger dropped away when she realized that people are doing the best they can based on their life experience and the way they were raised. There is such value in taking stock and getting curious about our perspectives in life.

What's the source?

When diagnosed with thyroid cancer, Nickolette asked herself, *What's the source?* She let go of arguing and fighting, and she started to pay attention. She in essence welcomed the cancer into her ecosystem and sat with it. From sitting with it she learned about herself. She learned that she was holding on to thoughts, feelings, and emotions that no longer served her. It took Nickolette two bouts with her cancer until she listened to the message to slow down and embrace the moment. Take time to sit and explore the challenging situations you find yourself in and see what you might discover.

Expose yourself to diversity

Jennifer Garbin's belief system transformed significantly in her journey to answer her calling. Her mind was first opened to the possibility of a different way of thinking when the Baptist minister said to her, "God uses all kinds of people for all kinds of things." Then over and over again she exposed herself to people and experiences that made her question the beliefs that she was raised with. Rather than holding on to her beliefs so tightly, she was open to questioning them and welcoming into her ecosystem the possibility that what she held as a truth may not be. It can be challenging to meet someone with a different belief system than us.

Our beliefs arise from our life experiences. If we were born in a different place, at a different time, to different parents, our beliefs and life experiences would be significantly different than they are right now. Being open to questioning our beliefs is important to growing into the full expression of ourselves. Getting in the habit of asking yourself, *Is it true? Are there other possibilities that may be just as true?* opens your mind to other possibilities, other perspectives, and the richness that diversity offers. When Jennifer let go of the labels that she placed on herself and others, she was able to embrace a different truth, one that aligned more with who she was.

Step 4. Nurture Yourself

> 66 *Don't be hard on yourself. Nobody else knows what they are doing.* 99
> CHRISTINE DERNEDERLANDEN

Create an environment that supports you—practise self-compassion, create a nurturing space, and surround yourself with people who nurture your becoming.

A plant that is not nurtured, that is not exposed to the right amount of the sun's energy, the right amount of water, and the right amount of nutrients from the soil is not going to thrive. In order to thrive, we have to feel nurtured. Some of us are lucky to be born into a nurturing environment, and we innately understand how to create a nurturing environment for ourselves; others are not so lucky and need to learn what that looks like.

When we are driving toward a goal or becoming so focused on doing, we can sometimes forget to look after ourselves. It is not possible to continue at peak performance without taking time for ourselves. Both Evelyn Encalada Grez and Christine Dernederlanden were in the middle of retreats when I spoke with them. After her husband died, Sandi Stride went to Bali to start her next becoming. Evelyn talked about taking retreats when she felt overwhelmed. When she retreats, she collects all her energy back in and takes time to reconnect with herself and what her spirit wants. Christine focused on what she needed to renew and replenish herself so she could continue her work.

Create a nurturing mind

66 *Be conscious that we can control our imagery rather than our imagery controlling us. It then becomes a tool for us, rather than the enemy.* 99

KAMINI JAIN

Be aware how you speak to yourself. Both Kamini Jain and Paddy Torsney spoke about how to create a supportive mind. Kamini spoke of switching her mind to be more self-congratulatory as she moved into a competition. Being more self-congratulatory allowed her body to flow. Paddy reassured herself with comforting words as the challenges of travelling solo through Europe unfolded.

Creating a nurturing mind starts with just noticing how you speak to yourself. We all have that critical voice within us. Our mind has our best interests at heart—it wants us to survive. We can choose to argue with it or worse yet believe it, or we can treat it like we would our best friend and find out what's up with it, reassure it by saying things like: *You're okay, you will be all right, you have worked through similar challenges before.* Perhaps some understanding and compassion is all that is needed. Dr. Kristen Neff, a researcher and self-compassion evangelist, suggests the following when you feel triggered:

1. Place your hands over your heart.
2. Acknowledge what you are feeling.
3. Talk to yourself like you are talking to your best friend.
4. Ask yourself what you need.

So it might sound like this: "Sweetheart, I can see you are frustrated. It is okay to feel frustrated. This situation is frustrating. I am so sorry you have to go through this right now. You will get through it. You have felt this way before and you have moved through it. What can I do for you? How can I help?" You may also want to reread Paddy's story. She provides examples of how to reassure and encourage yourself in stressful situations.

We can have a tendency to look at how far we still have to go, rather than how far we have come. When Lisa Belanger graduated with her PhD, her mother presented her with a gift that was all about celebrating her success. Lisa's mother created a scrapbook with "Dr. Lisa" on the front, and inside were pages and pages of Lisa's accomplishments, including photographs and newspaper articles. The book provides a tangible record that Lisa can look at to celebrate her accomplishments. It's definitely a great resource to look at if your critical mind decides to move in for a while. We all have accomplishments that need to be recognized and celebrated. Take some time to really reflect on your accomplishments thus far in life and celebrate yourself.

Remember that others need to be celebrated too. Always take a moment to really appreciate the people in your life who have made you who you are, who have supported or encouraged you in some way or made a difference in your life. It is one thing to feel that appreciation in your heart. It is quite another thing to tell someone how much they mean to you and what you appreciate about them. Notice what happens to how you feel when you do let people know what they mean to you.

Meditation is a practice that many of the women I interviewed use to support their minds. There are many different ways to meditate. You can choose a point of focus like focusing on your breath or a mantra of some kind. You can practise mindfulness by letting go of judgment and noticing with all your senses what is happening within you and around you. You could try guided mediations. The trick to meditation is to find what works for you, and it can start with just one conscious breath. If you would like to give it a try, you can download a guided meditation from my website: www.AlisonBraithwaite.com/In-Her-Own-Words.

There were times in Yasmine's life where the simple practice of prayer fed her. Her description of prayer is magical:

> The call to prayer is beautiful. It is gorgeous. You hear the Azan, the call to prayer, and you hear this beautiful chant. It is about stop, go and wash, your face, your hands up to your elbows, wash your feet, you wash your mouth and you feel a sense of freshness and then you go to wherever you can pray. If you can't go to the mosque you just go to your room or somewhere private and you just give yourself five minutes to just regroup. There is nothing better than that.

There is such ritual in this. Prayer may not be your thing, but the ritual of taking five minutes to regroup is a practice that can nurture your mind and spirit. Prayer is definitely a practice that Jennifer Garbin uses to create her thriving life.

Talking to a professional is an important way to support your mind. We all have moments when we need help. If your friends and family aren't moving you forward, maybe it's time to talk to a professional therapist, coach, or counsellor.

Self-expression is a way to nurture ourselves. It is a launching pad into a thriving life. What does self-expression mean to you? Laüra Hollick expresses herself through art. Laura Kooji through movement. Jane Hanlon gardens. Christine Dernederlanden writes and speaks. Writing about her brother's death shifted Christine into her thriving self. What is your soul longing to express?

Nurture your physical health

> 66 *Yoga is my medicine.* 99
> LISA BELANGER

Each of the women I interviewed had practices to support their physical health. Things that support your physical body also support the mind. Nickolette Reid loves kickboxing and yoga. Kamini, of course, loves to be on the water paddling. Laüra Hollick walks every day in nature. Jane Hanlon works in the garden and spends time in nature. Janet Nezon, of course, eats a Rainbow Plate. Chris rows and cross-country skis.

Surround yourself with nurturing people

> 66 *People are amazing and I think they are the most important piece of our ecosystem.* 99
> SHEENA REPATH

Jocelyn Mercer surrounded herself with friends who would stand for her as she allowed herself to feel the heartbreak she had held in for so long. Mary-Kate Gilbertson built a supportive community around her. Sheena had a father who advocated for her. Paddy relied on the help of strangers as she navigated around Europe. As Jennifer Garbin said, "To be a human being is to be in relationship." The relationships you are in are a reflection of who you are and the potential of who you are becoming.

Jody Steinhauer has a strong network around her. When she launches into something new, she finds role models to emulate. When she was becoming a mother, she looked to find mothers she admired. She took pieces from each of the women to help create the mother she wanted to be. When she needs guidance, she asks for help. Jody stresses the importance of asking for help and expects her team to reach out and ask for help when they need it. Devon found a role model in Kendal Netmaker, who was just a few steps ahead of her in his business. Jane Hanlon had a living room full of activist role models as she grew up.

Nurturing space

> 66 *The key to anything is to know who and where your support groups are and where your safe places are in the world.* 99
>
> LAURA KOOJI

The space that surrounds us can support our well-being. Even in a crowded workplace it is possible to add one thing that when you look at it makes you feel supported. For Jane Hanlon, the texture and colours of a garden and of nature nurture her. Lisa Belanger described the chair she curls up in to journal. Devon Fiddler left the school that she was attending to finish high school in her home community. That change was a huge step into choosing a nurturing space for herself and choosing to create her thriving life.

Step 5. Grow

> 66 *Understand how to be comfortable*
> *with the uncomfortable.* 99
>
> LISA BELANGER

You can't grow unless you take action. I used to buy into the idea of acting boldly, of being fearless in every step I took. Some of the things I have done in my life may have seemed bold and fearless—like standing up for what I believe in, quitting my job to write a book, going to live in Costa Rica, going to Peru on my own without a plan—and yet these were things that I felt called to do. They were easy for me. They were not bold or fearless. They were a bit uncomfortable. Growing does not require bold steps, it can happen in baby steps in the direction you want to go. As Lisa Belanger said, it is about understanding "how to be comfortable with the uncomfortable." We can't grow until we act and take even one small step beyond who we are today and toward who we are becoming. When you become comfortable with the uncomfortable, your movement forward will appear bold and fearless to others.

Alignment

When we are in alignment with who we are, life flows more smoothly. To be in alignment is to act from the place of your true nature. Fear drops away when you step into the fullness of your true nature.

Sometimes it takes being totally misaligned to step onto the path of alignment. Chris Hartmann was misaligned with finance and yet it provided her with the resources to learn and master pottery. Devon Fiddler worked in her community in a few jobs that were not in full alignment with who she was and yet those jobs provided her with the knowledge and opportunities she needed to launch herself into entrepreneurship. Lisa Belanger was totally misaligned with the idea of making academics her career and she knew it. It took her husband to ask her, "If you could do anything, *anything*, what would you do?" for her to align her life's work with who she is.

Imagine yourself already there

Nickolette Reid said it best: "If I can see it in my head and feel it in my heart, it is already mine." This is where the magic begins. Jocelyn Mercer would close her eyes and call up her white room and begin to imagine. As Laüra Hollick said, "Our imagination is our access to a new reality." Put your imagination to work and take steps to nurture your creativity.

Commitment

Without committing to something, it is impossible to move forward no matter how much we wish it to happen. It starts with making a commitment to a direction. Devon Fiddler's commitment to her businesses happened the moment she took a picture with Kendal Netmaker at the business plan competition and said to herself, *Yes, I'm going to do this.* Chris Hartmann's moment of commitment happened when her neighbours put a For Sale sign on their lawn so they could move back to Niagara. It was that twang of envy she felt that spurred her commitment to move to Niagara and make it work.

Making a commitment today doesn't mean you are married to it the rest of your life. Sheena Repath committed to being a pediatric surgeon. She started to follow that path until she discovered it really didn't align with who she was, and she pivoted. Christine Dernederlanden sees her life as a bit of an experiment. She made a commitment to being a TV reporter, to being the manager of a lingerie store, to starting a used toy store, and to running the family business. Christine has lived by the words of Paddy Torsney: "Don't be afraid to try something out." Gloria Roheim McRae definitely lived Paddy's advice as well. She had had twenty-one jobs by the time she was twenty-five years old. When she had a vision of something she wanted to try, she tried it. With each of these experiments, Christine and Gloria learned about themselves and got clearer on what they really wanted. All that experimenting created who they are today.

Start where you are

Sometime the gap between who we are and who we dream of being seems like a deep gorge full of impassable vegetation. Even though that gap seems impassable, the ideal place to begin your journey is from where you are and the best time to start is right now. You may hear yourself saying, *I don't know how.* Don't fool yourself, you know the way. Pivot yourself in the direction you are going, ask yourself what is your next aligned step, and take that step, no matter how tiny it is. It may be imperceptible to others, but it will be clear to you and it will open the possibility for the next step forward.

Sheena Repath's step was to declare she wanted to be a pediatric surgeon to her dad. The next step was to act into it by seeing the guidance counsellor at school. The next steps are so doable when we just get quiet and still and ask. The answer may not come immediately, but it will come. Sometimes I wake up with my next step. Sometimes it finds me when I am riding my bike. Sometimes it finds me in nature.

Remember, you can just ask someone else. Janet Nezon shared these wise words with me: "The world's greatest teachers are right in front of you, all around us. We just have to be open to listen for them." Chris Hartmann lived this when she got in her car and visited all the potters in her community to introduce herself and tell them she was opening a studio to teach students.

Setting goals

Do you like to set goals? Mary-Kate Gilbertson shared her goal-setting approach with me. Her approach may empower you to achieve the results you are looking for:

RESULTS
What do you want to achieve?
This goes further than the tasks you want to accomplish. It is about the impact that you would like to have. It is defining the change you wish to see (in the world, your community, yourself) as a consequence of your achieving the goal.

PURPOSE
Why do you want to accomplish that goal?
Understanding your why is a powerful step. Ethnographer Simon Sinek has done amazing work about the impact of starting with why. I encourage you to watch his TED Talk.

CONTEXT
How do you want to feel as you create the results?
Gloria Roheim McRae is an advocate of context and would ask this question differently. She would ask, "What is the experience you are hungry for?" Understanding the feeling you would like to experience allows you to be open to alternative ways for the experience to unfold.

Laüra Hollick uses art as her way to plan her next steps. She creates her future self with colour, textile, sketching, and painting. She expresses her soul onto the page and the manifesting of her next becoming begins there. Sandi Stride developed a ten-year plan when she wanted to move forward into her next becoming.

Trust your own approach. Whether you paint, write, create goals or ten-year plans, make it be in alignment with who you are.

Trust

You are the creator of your own becoming. Trust yourself. In the words of Gloria Roheim McRae: "You are more wondrous and intuitive than you think." Never lose sight of that. Laüra Hollick spoke of the "wholehearted yes" she feels within herself that tells her she is on the right track. Neuroscientists confirm that intuition exists and that it is a whole-body experience quite separate from the mind.

Start to practise using your intuition. Listen to what your whole body is telling you. Pay attention to when your mind kicks in and questions your intuition. Always question the thoughts. Remember that intuition is reliable but it's not 100 percent reliable. Your health, your stress level, trauma, alcohol, and drugs can affect your intuition. Your intuition will also be affected by the culture you grew up in and your life experience so far. Intuition is a muscle worth exercising. Take time to experiment with it.

Persist

Remember Jocelyn Mercer's tattoo: *discipline equals freedom.* Persistence is not always easy. It takes courage, discipline, and consistent action to create your next becoming. Chris Hartmann persisted with pottery lessons. Paddy Torsney persisted through the challenges of travelling alone in Europe. Kamini Jain persisted with her training to be able to realize her dream of representing Canada in the Olympics. What could you accomplish if you persisted?

Allow

View yourself as an ecosystem. Don't fight yourself. Sometimes persistence can turn into a struggle. In nature, there is a right time for everything. While one rose blossoms, others are still buds. Some things take time. When persistence becomes a struggle, it may be time to take a step back and allow rather than force things to happen. Honour your own rhythm and your own timing.

Several years ago I attended a Qigong weekend retreat. The Qigong master gave me a rose and asked me to see what I could learn from it. The rose was a deep red colour, and its smell was enchanting. The velvety red petals were tightly wound into a bud. I went back to my room to explore the rose and see what it had to teach me. For whatever reason, I decided to start peeling the petals off the rose and spreading them around me. The more petals I removed, the more difficult it became to remove the next one. As I moved into the centre of the rose, the petals started to rip and I continued to force my way to the centre of the rose to see what message it had for me. I was left with a flowerless stem and went to sleep without understanding the message from the rose.

I woke up with the realization that I could have nurtured the rose open. I could have put it in a vase with some water and a little sugar and enjoyed watching it open one graceful moment at a time. Once it had fully unfolded, those beautiful petals would have dropped one by one as they surrendered themselves into their next becoming. So we have a choice: be patient and nurture ourselves into being or struggle and force what we believe we are meant to become.

Adapt

Nature is in a constant state of adapting. Plants adapt themselves to the movement of the sun and chameleons adapt their colour to the environment they are in. Life can throw all sorts of challenges at us, which may appear to get in the way of what we want. When you feel challenged, look for a way to adapt. Try a different way. Sometimes we are so set on a direction we miss the signs that are pointing us toward something different.

When I interviewed Chris Hartmann, she was in the process of adapting how she made money. She was shifting from selling her pottery at arts and crafts fairs to selling it online.

———

ONCE YOU HAVE spiralled through the steps, celebrate your growth and welcome your next journey through the upward spiral of your life. Refine your nature. Root into the new expression of yourself. Ask, *What matters to me now? What principles am I living into now?* They may be the same, they may have transformed, they may have tweaked just a bit. As you grow, you may find a new belief limiting you. Then again, it may just be the same belief that transformed on your last journey through the spiral of your life that needs to be shifted again. With that shift, you open yourself up to grow into the next expression of yourself. You may become aware of new ways to nurture and support yourself, and the people you surround yourself with may be slightly different. The environment that nurtures you may also change. Pay attention and make the shifts you need to grow again, then again and again. Live into the upward spiral of your unique way of being.

5

A FINAL
WORD

> *Everything that we have ever thought of or wanted already exists. It's just, can we find the magnet to pull it toward us?*

GLORIA ROHEIM MCRAE

I HAVE LEARNED SO much from interviewing these women and diving deeply into their stories. Their experiences reverberate within me as I move forward to my next becoming. Their words of wisdom have me reflecting back on my own experiences. They have taught me what it really means to nurture myself and how important it is to be in alignment with who I am. What I take away from all of this is to:

- Notice when I am feeling the need to shut down part of myself to fit in. Instead, I will course-correct so that doesn't happen.
- Be solid in who I am, yet always curious about the beliefs I hold about myself and other people that could be getting in my way.
- Sit with my strong emotions, get curious about what lies beneath them, and act on their message.
- Hold space for the strong emotions of others and get curious about what lies beneath them.
- Let go of my need to rescue by holding other people capable and setting boundaries around my time and my resources so that I protect my energy and my mental and physical health.
- Say "no" clearly and unapologetically or "no, not now, perhaps

Thursday," if that is the case.

- Let others fight their own battles.
- Speak to myself compassionately and consciously look for the things that I do well and celebrate those things more.
- Stop looking for appreciation and affirmation from others, especially not from those who have no idea or no intention of providing it.
- Surround myself with people who support me and want the best for me, people who nurture my soul.
- Allow myself and the people around me to make mistakes, trusting that only good will come from those failures.
- Speak out about how I really feel—so often, feeling hurt masquerades as anger. Learn to say clearly, "That hurt me."
- Stop judging people against who I want them to be. Instead, accept them for who they are. Only they can change themselves. Don't expend my energy by trying to change them.
- Read the signs of where I am being pulled to go and move in that direction.
- Remember that we are all so interconnected—what we do to others, we do to ourselves; what we do to ourselves, we do to others.

If I had learned all this wisdom earlier, would I have had the tools to happily stay where I was or would I have left a lot sooner than I did? It doesn't matter. Everything played out exactly as it needed to. As a result, I was motivated to look for answers, reach out to women, hear their stories, and share their wisdom with all of you. In the process, I changed myself and stepped into my next becoming.

All that said, the world is crying out for each of us to reach our full expression and help pull others into their own beingness. Imagine a thriving world, dreamed and created from a place of wholeness, where every person, every being, has stepped out of what is holding them frozen in time and fully stepped into their place of dreaming and realizing a thriving world.

The world needs us. The world needs each of us to share our gifts and fully live the purpose that we were born into. As we each begin to fully show up in the world, it behooves us to help others do the same. So why would you dream, if you're not going to manifest your dreams into reality? This is where you take the driver's seat. This is where you start to take responsibility for your life.

It is your time to shine. To help you, I have summarized all the amazing lessons that I have learned as I wrote this book in a declaration for a thriving life. It is a simple reference for you to stay in the upward spiral of life. My wish for you is that your life thrives precisely the way you desire it.

MY DECLARATION
FOR A THRIVING LIFE

I N EVERY MOMENT, I choose to step out of the chaos that may surround me in life and step into the stillness and space between my thoughts. My thriving self is the observer who lies under my survival mind. I create myself as an ecosystem with all parts ultimately wanting to work together. As an ecosystem, I don't fight myself. I accept all of myself.

My thriving self is the full expression of my true nature. I root into my true nature. With ease and grace, I make mulch of what no longer serves me, releasing it into the earth to transform into what I need to support and nurture myself.

I nurture myself to thrive physically, emotionally, mentally, and spiritually. I surround myself with a nurturing community of people who stand for me to thrive and grow. I create a nurturing environment around me that supports me to thrive. I retreat to call all my energies back to me, reconnect with my true nature, and discover what my spirit most desires.

I act in alignment with who I am and what matters most to me in the world. I live in an upward spiral of being and becoming, of creating and re-creating myself.

Every day I remind myself that I am amazing. I am capable. I am unique and am worth celebrating. Then I go out and shine my brilliant nature where it is needed most to create a thriving world.

Acknowledgements

I HAD NO IDEA what I would experience as I wrote this book. I had no idea how long it would take. I wanted to share stories so that no one would have to experience the unravelling that I had experienced. Little did I know how important the experience of writing and the experience of unravelling would be to me. In my writing, I have danced through anger, frustration, confusion into letting go and forgiveness—forgiveness of others but, most importantly, forgiveness of myself.

I have dived deeply into the depths of my soul and have been guided by stories that on the surface seemed so straightforward and such a gift. As I tried to live the wisdom that was shared with me, I realized the layers and layers of gifts that were woven into each of the stories that were so graciously and openly shared with me. I have been transformed through writing. I have met my screen almost every day and found my voice and myself.

I am so grateful to the women who shared their stories with me—Laüra Hollick, Evelyn Encalada Grez, Jennifer Garbin, Laura Kooji, Yasmine Kandil, Jocelyn Mercer, Gloria Roheim McRae, Devon Fiddler, Lisa Belanger, Nickolette Reid, Christine Dernederlanden, Kamini Jain, Paddy Torsney, Jane Hanlon,

Jody Steinhauer, Sheena Repath, Janet Nezon, Mary-Kate Gilbertson, Sandi Stride, and Chris Hartmann. I carry a piece of you in my heart and always will. As I type each of your names, I am struck with the power of who you are and how amazing the world is as a result of you all being in it. So often the names of women who have changed the world get lost, and yet each one of us transforms our little piece of the world by just being who we are. Thank you for opening the door to my understanding of that. I am so grateful to each of you for being so open about your lives and your struggles. It made me realize I am not alone and that anything is possible when we find our own rhythm and honour it, live it. Life really is a poem that we write each day, and I am grateful for the life experiences I have had and how they have guided me to this moment.

I was so blessed to have had Alia Ziesman read my first draft. Her enthusiasm for the essence of the book was very reassuring. Her enthusiastic advice was to include my own story. I never understood how difficult that would be for me and what was required of me to include me in the book. It was Alia's words that began my next journey into myself, and I unravelled myself and took an honest look. I wrote and rewrote my story, and it took more than a year to share what I have.

Ellen Rodger read the next version of my book. Her questions and thoughts at times annoyed me and yet created a clarity in my words I would not have reached without her challenging what I said and how I said it.

Support has come from the strangest places. My mail carrier regularly asks about the book, which I find heartening. So many women got excited about the idea of this book; when I shared what I was doing, theirs eyes would light up, and I am so grateful for that. Those lit-up eyes and encouragements got me through the moments when I heard, "Stop writing," "Who is going to read the book?" or "Who is going to buy this book?" from myself or others. I can't remember who it was, but I am so grateful to the first person who said, "I will buy that book." It has served as a constant reminder that yes, someone will buy this book—I just had to finish writing it.

I am grateful for my nieces and nephews. I have always felt recognized, seen, and loved by you, even if one of you thinks I'm overdue. A turning point for me that made this book less of a possibility and more of a reality was when one of my nieces asked me to speak at a Women in Leadership Conference that she had organized. It was there that the door of opportunity opened and I met Sheena Repath, who was instrumental in connecting me with so many of the women in this book.

I am deeply appreciative of all the women in my life who have stood by me, challenged me, and grown with me. I hold a place in my heart for the Sisters of the Dancing Deer for welcoming me into their sisterhood for an evening of sharing that opened me to the magic and ceremony that life holds for us. For my sisters who listened to me as I questioned myself, to my friends who sat with me over tea and coffee or walked in the woods with me and kept me grounded—I am so appreciative of each of you. To my friends on Facebook, some of whom I have never met, I appreciate the love and support you have provided me through my journey home to myself. You are all such courageous souls. I also want to acknowledge my father, who unwittingly created a daughter who dances to a different beat and yet stands by my crazy decisions to throw the "family success formula" to the wind and see where it lands. Though my mother is no longer alive, so much of what I have written is as a result of her struggle back to herself, back to the love we all are searching for.

I am most grateful to my husband, Tim, who just allows me to be me. He has stood by me, cradled me, loved me, and watched me unfold. I feel his loving support for whatever happens, for whatever is next.

And I am so grateful to you, the reader. I can't wait to hear your story.

Appendix 1

1. How would you describe yourself?
2. How does your culture(s) use dreaming?
3. How do you use dreaming in your life?
4. How did you learn to dream? How did you learn about dreaming/visualization?
5. What is the world/life you are dreaming?
6. Tell me your story. What are the turning points in your life that brought you to this point?
7. What tools do you use to dream that world/life?
8. I heard an interview with Malala Yousafzai. When talking about her father, she said, "For him I was special. I think every girl is special and every person is special but my father recognized me because there were many other girls who were special but their parents did not recognize them . . . " When you were young, was there someone in your life who recognized you, someone who saw you for who you truly are—your essence?
9. What did you have to overcome/heal to accomplish what you have—to dream the world as you have?
10. How do you know you are on the right track?
11. What do you do when things are not working for you?

12. What inspires you?
13. Did you ever get in your own way?
14. How did you get out of your way?
15. What was life like for you when you were young?
16. What advice do you have for young women about creating a successful life?
17. What questions do you think are important for a young woman to ask herself as she learns to dream her future?

Appendix 2

THE SEVEN GRANDFATHER TEACHINGS

LAURA KOOJI DESCRIBED how the Seven Grandfather Teachings guided her life through dark times and have helped her to navigate the world. The seven teachings are interconnected and interdependent. You can't embrace one without embracing all the others. The teachings form the roots essential for growing a thriving community. They are taught through observing the intrinsic behaviours and characters of the animals found in nature. Each of the principles is demonstrated by a specific animal. A wonderful resource I found with a basic description of the Seven Grandfather Teachings is An Ojibwe People's Resource at ojibweresources.weebly.com.

These are not my stories to tell. In this age where sacred knowledge and culture is being appropriated without the consent of the people who belong to that culture, I consulted with Laura about how I have presented these teachings. What she wanted me to emphasize in presenting this information is that these teachings are learned by experience. They are learned by going to Anishinaabe events, hearing and experiencing the teachings. These stories are not something you can learn from a book.

What Laura offered in her story is only a glimpse of the Seven Grandfather Teachings. I would encourage you to do some more research into the teachings if you feel called to and find an Indigenous teacher who may be willing to share through experience the depth of these sacred teachings.

Appendix 3

THE THIRTEEN GRANDMOTHER
MOON TEACHINGS

THE THIRTEEN GRANDMOTHER Moon Teachings also emerge from the wisdom of the natural world that surrounds us. They share the wisdom of what it means to be nature and recognize the intrinsic connection that women have to the earth. The Grandmother Teachings describe how to honour the cycles of the moon and live in the natural rhythm of nature.

There are thirteen moons each year that in essence form the calendar, and there are Thirteen Grandmother Teachings that coincide with those moons. By looking at the names of the moons you can see how they relate to what is happening in nature at that time of the year. The teachings provide guidance on how to align your life to the energy of that time of year. These teachings are sacred teachings.

As Laura Kooji reminds us, these teachings are the traditional knowledge of the Anishinaabe people and are learned through experience. Those experiences cannot happen by just reading the words on a page. If you would like to explore the depth of the messages in these teachings, go to Anishinaabe events or seek out an Indigenous teacher who may be willing to share their teachings. An Indigenous teacher will ensure you receive the teachings from a place that is grounded in authenticity.

When researching the Grandmother Teachings, I noticed that most Anishinaabe websites refer to *Thirteen Grandmother Moon Teachings* by Arlene Barry, from her series of compiled teachings "Kinoomaadiewinan Anishinaabe Bimaadinzinwin," Book Two, pages 17 and 18. If you search this reference, you will find the moons explained in Arlene's words. These teachings are hers to share, not mine. I encourage you to explore Arlene's explanations of the moons. Her words may entice you to explore your own moon rhythm.

Appendix 4

VORTEX DANCE WORKSHEET

THE WORKSHEET ON the following page will help you with your awareness of the roles you might be playing that are helping to keep you stuck.

When I am playing oppressor...

My name is: ....

My body feels: ....

The situations that trigger me are:

....

What I get out of it is: ....

What I am looking for is: ....

The people I like to dance with are:

....

When I am playing victim...

My name is: ....

My body feels: ....

The situations that trigger me are:

....

What I get out of it is: ....

What I am looking for is: ....

The people I like to dance with are:

....

When I am playing rescuer...

My name is: ....

My body feels: ....

The situations that trigger me are:

....

What I get out of it is: ....

What I am looking for is: ....

The people I like to dance with are:

....

Appendix 5

IF YOU ARE looking for more resources to assist you on your journey, please visit www.AlisonBraithwaite.com/In-Her-Own-Words and you will discover:

1. How to Step Out of the Vortex
   * A guide to provide you with more support to step out of the downward vortex.

2. A Guided Meditation
   * A meditation to learn how to take that one conscious breath and to breathe into your true nature.

3. My Declaration for a Thriving Life
   * A downloadable PDF version of the declaration that you can use as a daily reference.

4. Workshops and groups that allow you to dive more deeply into creating your thriving life.

Appendix 6

NOT ALL THE women I interviewed offered specific resources.
Those who did are listed here.

EVELYN ENCALADA GREZ
* *The House of the Spirits* by Isabel Allende
* *The Great Work of Your Life: A Guide for the Journey to Your True
  Calling* by Stephen Cope

MARY-KATE GILBERTSON
* *An Astronaut's Guide to Life on Earth* by Chris Hadfield
* *Poke the Box* by Seth Godin
* *The Power of Just Doing Stuff* by Rob Hopkins

JANE HANLON
* *An Inconvenient Truth* by Al Gore (either the book or the film)
* *The First Follower* video

LAURA KOOJI
* *Big Magic* by Elizabeth Gilbert
* *Rising Strong* by Brené Brown

JOCELYN MERCER
- *Key to Living the Law of Attraction* by Jack Canfield (or any other of his books)
- *The Secret Book of Kings* by Yochi Brandes
- *The Brain That Changes Itself* by Norman Doidge
- *The Secret* by Rhonda Byrne (either the book or the film)

GLORIA ROHEIM MCRAE
- TED Talks
- *Tears to Triumph: The Spiritual Journey from Suffering to Enlightenment* by Marianne Williamson (or any of her other books)
- *The Desire Map* by Danielle LaPorte

SHEENA REPATH
- *The Passion Test* by Chris and Janet Attwood

About the Contributors

Lisa Belanger

www.lisabelanger.ca

LISA BELANGER IS a speaker, author, health advocate, and founder of Knight's Cabin Cancer Retreats. She holds a PhD in behavioural medicine and is a certified exercise physiologist. She is CEO of ConsciousWorks, a boutique consulting firm that shows leader how insights from behavioural science can strategically improve habits of both corporate leaders and their employees.

Christine Dernederlanden

www.robertspress.ca

CHRISTINE DERNEDERLANDEN IS a certified trauma services specialist and has been recognized internationally for her work. She is an award-winning author of *Where's Robert?*, the grief kit that aided more than six thousand families affected by 9/11, *H.U.G.S.: Helping Children Understand Grief,* and *Where Is My Courage?*

Devon Fiddler

www.shenative.com · @DevyFiddler

DEVON FIDDLER IS a social entrepreneur and the founder and chief changemaker at SheNative Goods Inc. She has a bachelor's degree in Aboriginal public administration from the University of Saskatchewan and has completed numerous leadership, economic development, entrepreneurship, and business certificate programs.

Jennifer Garbin

@SBPastorJen

JENNIFER GARBIN IS the lead pastor of Sugarbush Christina Church (Disciples of Christ) in Guelph, Ontario. She has a doctor of ministry from Emmanuel College, University of Toronto. Her area of study focused on exploring how Christian emerging adults who don't actively attend worship are living out their faith.

Mary-Kate Gilbertson

www.kaboomconsulting.ca

MARY-KATE GILBERTSON IS a passionate community builder dedicated to catalyzing resilient, connected communities. She has more than twenty years of experience in environmental work and is the owner of Kaboom Consulting. She has a bachelor of environmental science from the University of Plymouth.

Evelyn Encalada Grez

www.evelynencalada.com · @professor_evy

EVELYN ENCALADA GREZ is an adjunct university professor, transnational community organizer, and labour researcher. She teaches in work and labour studies at York University and also online for the University of British Columbia. She founded the award-winning collective Justicia/Justice for Migrant Workers (J4MW) that is at the forefront of the migrant rights movement in this country.

Jane Hanlon

JANE HANLON STUDIED applied horticulture and horticultural business services at Niagara College. She was the founding executive director of Greening Niagara. As an active volunteer, Jane has been involved with the Niagara District Council of women since 2005, served as a director of Land Care Niagara, and is now the environmental convener of the Provincial Council of Women of Ontario.

Chris Hartmann
www.athirdspacepottery.com

CHRIS HARTMANN HAS a diploma in cooking from George Brown College and studied history and French at Glendon College, the University Laval in Quebec. Throughout her twenty-five-year career in finance, Chris studied pottery at various studios. She studied under Mary Philpott of Verdant Tile Studio and Sister Helen at Studio on the Hill. Chris is the founder of A Third Space Pottery Studio and is a member of the Hamilton Potters Guild.

Laüra Hollick
www.laurahollick.com

LAÜRA HOLLICK IS an award-winning artist, creative spiritual entrepreneur, and lover of our earth. She is known as the Soul Art® Shaman. Laüra is the creator of Soul Art®, a unique creative practice that awakens our innate healing abilities, unleashes our creative genius, and taps into our intuition superpowers.

Kamini Jain

www.rightangleperformance.com

AN OLYMPIC PADDLER with eleven World Cup medals, Kamini Jain now coaches. She brings to her coaching thirty years of success as both an athlete and a coach. Kamini has a master of science degree in biology from Simon Fraser University and a master's degree in leadership from Royal Roads.

Yasmine Kandil

YASMINE KANDIL HAS a bachelor's degree in theatre from the American University in Cairo and her master of fine arts degree in theatre and her PhD in applied theatre from the University of Victoria. She is now an assistant professor of drama in education and applied theatre at Brock University, St. Catharines, Ontario.

Laura Kooji

LAURA KOOJI STUDIED visual and performing arts at Humber College and fitness and wellness leadership at Mohawk College. Her work in social services included supporting immigrant women and incarcerated women. Her current role is a youth adviser for Indigenous students. She also enjoys public speaking, writing, and the performing arts.

Gloria Roheim McRae

www.gloriaroheim.com · @GloriaRoheim

GLORIA ROHEIM MCRAE is an author, strategist, and speaker. She is the co-founder and chief strategic officer of Wedge15 Inc. Gloria earned her bachelor of arts degree at McGill University and master's degree in international affairs from the University of Toronto. She speaks four languages fluently, is a regular *Huffington Post* columnist, and is a HuffPost Live commentator.

Jocelyn Mercer

www.notedwithlove.com · @jocelynmercer11

JOCELYN MERCER IS an executive producer, director, story-teller, and one-half of CJ Creative—a company that creates and builds character-driven digital brands that capture new audiences, connect with target markets, and maximize revenue on online platforms such as YouTube and Facebook. CJ Creative was recently listed in the coveted "5 To Watch" feature in *Playback Magazine*.

Janet Nezon

www.rainbowplate.com

JANET NEZON IS founder and program director of Rainbow Plate. With a bachelor of nutritional science and a master's degree in health science from the University of Toronto, Janet's roots are in science and health promotion. She is an engaging and innovative educator, change agent, and speaker.

Nickolette Reid

www.nickolettereid.com · @NixReid

NICKOLETTE REID IS currently the general merchandise manager at Gap Inc. She studied marketing at the University of Toronto and image communication and bookkeeping at George Brown College. She provides seminars, etiquette coaching, and image development workshops at the Toronto District School Board and has run her own image consulting business.

Sheena Repath

www.makingshthappen.com

SHEENA REPATH IS founder and chief of making sh*t happen, MSH District Inc., co-founder and chief inspirer at Making Sh*t

Happen, and president and founder of Ideal Samplers Inc., and is on the advisory board of Startup Fashion Week. She studied fashion design and merchandising at Fanshawe College. She describes herself as a product-hacking, idea-unleashing people connector.

Jody Steinhauer
www.jodysteinhauer.com

JODY STEINHAUER STUDIED fashion merchandising at the International Academy of Fashion Merchandising and Design. She is founder, president, and chief bargain officer at the Bargain Group; a motivational speaker; and founder of Engage and Change, a national charity focusing on "good people working together for good people." Jody has won multiple awards, including Canadian Woman Entrepreneur of the Year and Canada's Top 40 under 40.

Sandi Stride

SANDI STRIDE IS the executive director of the Centre for Climate Change Management at Niagara College and was the founding president and CEO at Sustainable Hamilton Burlington. She has a bachelor of science degree in physical geography and biology from the University of Toronto and a master of business administration degree from the University of Western Ontario. Sandy worked in marketing and communications for several years before finding her way back to her desire for a more sustainable world.

Paddy Torsney

PADDY TORSNEY IS a former Member of the Parliament of Canada and is currently a permanent observer to the United

Nations and president of the New York office at Inter-Parliamentary Union. She has a bachelor of commerce degree from McGill University and experience working for government and public relations. She began her career working in the office of the Premier of Ontario.

About the Author

ALISON BRAITHWAITE IS an explorer and seeker. She has trekked to the base of Mount Everest, cycled in Patagonia, studied art in Costa Rica, and lived at a yoga centre. Her most challenging yet most worthwhile journeys have been those toward self-discovery. Her inward explorations have led her to yoga, meditation, art, writing, and coaching. Alison has a keen awareness of how incredibly interconnected the world is and believes if we each aligned ourselves with who we truly are, the world would be a better place. She is passionate about helping other women align with their true nature and prevent the possibility of them burning out. A former executive responsible for environmental performance and corporate social responsibility, Alison is now an executive coach with a master's degree in leadership from Royal Roads University. For more information please visit: **www.AlisonBraithwaite.com**